WAR-TORN SKIES
OF
GREAT BRITAIN

SURREY

IN THE
BATTLE OF BRITAIN

CONTENTS

First published 2007 by
Red Kite
PO Box 223,
Walton on Thames
Surrey, KT12 3YQ

www.redkitebooks.co.uk

Series editor
Simon W Parry

Design and layout by Steven J Postlethwaite
Printed in Malta by Progress Press.

ISBN 978-0-9554735-0-0

INTRODUCTION

The busy skies of Surrey that are now full of charter flights from Gatwick and international arrivals heading for Heathrow once echoed with the roar of engines and the clatter of machine-gun fire as young men fought to the death in Spitfires and Messerschmitts. The momentous battle for the skies over England, fought more than 65 years ago, is as important as the Battle of Hastings or the Spanish Armada, yet it is possible to walk around Surrey unaware that the Battle of Britain ever happened. Aircraft and bombs fell from the sky and men died across Surrey in the summer of 1940, yet few events have attracted permanent memorials.

This book records for the first time Surrey's decisive part in the legendary Battle of Britain; the devastating attacks on the airfields at Croydon, Kenley and Brooklands, and the battles fought overhead.

A chance remark in 1976 set me on a trail that dictated the course of my life from then on, "We used to play in hole where a German 'plane crashed in the war," a friend told me; that was all it took. Completely absorbed by the idea of being able to find a tangible reminder of the war, I set off to discover the German bomber, then its history, then the other aircraft that crashed in Surrey, and then all the Luftwaffe aircraft and airmen in Britain. After writing and publishing many aviation books over the past 30 years I finally decided to return to my 'roots' and do what I always said I would do one day; write a book about Surrey in the Battle of Britain.

I have been fortunate to have had the support of many historians who have contributed to this account; Colin Brown, Peter Cornwell, Steven Flower, Peter Foote, John Foreman, Larry Hickey, Dennis Knight and Philippa Wheeler among them. I am particularly grateful to Dennis Knight for his hospitality over the past 30 years, the many hours spent piecing together the events detailed here, and for permission to use his notes and sketches. Thanks also go to the many people who have helped me as I went in search of eyewitnesses. The accounts gathered many years ago have now been combined with written material to provide the most comprehensive account possible, yet there are still some events that defy comprehensive description. The precise location of some aircraft crash sites have evaded me, the circumstances of some combats are open to debate, so I invite anyone who can contribute to contact me via the publisher or by e-mail:

simon@redkitebooks.com

Simon Parry

Le Biot, France
February 2007

SURREY AIRFIELDS

BROOKLANDS

Famous as the home of British motor racing and flying, Brooklands was also home to two aircraft manufacturers, Vickers and Hawkers in the 1930s. By 1940 Vickers was producing Wellingtons and Hawkers assembling Hurricanes from components made at Kingston; both made tempting targets for the Luftwaffe.

A devastating raid on 4 September temporarily halted Wellington production, but the Hurricane assembly line was unaffected. No operational squadrons were based there.

CROYDON

Had been the 'Heathrow' of pre-war years since 1928 and was the busiest international airport in Europe. The Imperial Airways fleet of airliners was based there and aircraft of other nationalities visited on a daily basis until 30 August 1939, when all civilian operations stopped and the airfield became a satellite of Kenley. A few days later the Gladiators of No.615 Squadron arrived and military personnel began digging trenches and machine gun sites.

At the start of the Battle of Britain No.111 Squadron was based at Croydon equipped with Hurricanes. The airfield and the surrounding area were severely damaged on 15 August when attacked by Me110s, but it was operational again the following day. The battered Treble-One Squadron left on 19 August and was immediately replaced by 85 Squadron that was in action until 1 September. The Spitfires of 72 Squadron arrived, followed by the return of 111 Squadron on 2 September. No.605 Squadron swapped places with 85 Squadron on 8 September and, after the Spitfires left on 14 September, 605 became the sole occupant of Croydon until the end of the Battle.

FAIROAKS

The grass landing strip at Fairoaks opened in the 1930s and was run by General Aircraft Ltd on behalf of RAF Flying Training Command. A centre for the repair of Bristol aircraft was also based there. The pupils at the flying school used Tiger Moths for initial training during the Battle of Britain period, but no operational aircraft were based there.

GATWICK

In June 1936 Gatwick opened as purpose built airport, with the idea that it would one day become London's second airport, Croydon being the first. It had a revolutionary circular terminal allowing passengers to board their planes under cover and its own railway station giving fast access to London. Things did not go well for the ambitious airfield and its operating company when the biggest airlines continued to use Croydon and the Government selected Heston (close to what is now Heathrow) as London's second airport. Minor operators continued to use Gatwick and flying training schools operated from its runways until the outbreak of war when it was requisitioned by the RAF. During the Phoney War, with Croydon closed to them and Heston regarded as unsuitable, major airlines began to use the airfield until the real 'shooting war' started in May 1940. During the Battle of Britain it was a satellite to Kenley, but no operational fighter squadrons were based there.

KENLEY

The Kenley memorial erected inside one of the blast pens that protected fighters on the airfield.

The RAF station at Kenley came under the control of Fighter Command in 1936 and became a key part of London's defences as 'B' Sector HQ in 11 Group. The airfield was considered to be of such importance that it was heavily defended with machine-guns, 40mm Bofors guns and a couple of old 3 inch anti-aircraft guns. Famously, Kenley also had a rocket powered 'Parachute and Cable' device that would shoot a curtain of cables into the air in front of any attacker. Shelters were constructed for the personnel and blast pens to protect the aircraft. Two concrete runways had been laid to keep the fighters operational whatever the weather.

On 10 July 1940 the Hurricanes of No.615 Squadron and Spitfires of 64 Squadron were based at Kenley, but flew to advanced airfields near the coast each day. Kenley was all-but destroyed in the 18 August attack, but like Croydon, was ready to send out patrols by the following day.

No.64 Squadron was replaced by 616 Squadron and 615 Squadron by 253 at the end of August. Both squadrons were immediately in the thick of combat at the height of the Battle and suffered heavy losses. No.616 Squadron was withdrawn and replaced by 66 Squadron on 3 September, but stayed only a week before moving on and making way for the Hurricanes of No.501 Squadron. The two Hurricane squadrons remained at Kenley for the remainder of the Battle, not moving until January 1941.

REDHILL

Opened in 1934 by the Redhill Flying Club, the airfield was busy training both civilian and RAF pilots. By 1939 many RAF pilots were receiving basic training at Redhill on de Havilland Moths, yet just two months before war was declared the atmosphere was still relaxed enough to organise an airshow at which a swastika emblazoned FW200 Condor was displayed alongside a Hurricane and Wellington. When war was declared all the aircraft were moved away and Redhill became home to No.15 Elementary Flying Training School and also an evaluation centre for the many Polish airmen who had arrived in Britain. As the situation in France worsened the flying school was moved away and a series of RAF squadrons appeared. During the Battle of Britain, Blenheim night fighters of No. 600 Squadron were based there, but no Hurricanes or Spitfires.

The old airfield at Kenley is now a common; joggers circuit the perimeter track, but gliders still take to the sky from its runways.

The summer of 1940 has been referred to as 'that long, hot summer' but it was in reality no longer, nor hotter than any other English summer. According to official RAF doctrine the 'Battle of Britain' began on 10 July 1940, but it would be wrong to suggest that there had been little air activity over Surrey in the weeks and months before that date. Squadrons based at Surrey's two operational fighter stations, Kenley and Croydon, had been flying patrols over the Channel and in support of 'Operation Dynamo' the evacuation of the British Expeditionary Force from Dunkirk for months.

Aircraft from other stations passing overhead kept the skies of Surrey busy, either training, practicing dogfights or moving to forward airfields. On June 17th a Hawker Hurricane mysteriously crashed in flames at West Horsley during a flight from Tangmere in Sussex to North Weald in Essex. Its pilot, Flying Officer Leonid Ereminsky from No.56 Squadron died in the wreck and was buried at Whyteleafe Cemetery near to the airfield at Kenley.

Shortly after the 'official' start of the Battle of Britain the Spitfire equipped No.610 Squadron based at Biggin Hill, just across the county border in Kent, suffered two fatal accidents during training. On July 12th the Spitfire flown by Sergeant Sydney Ireland was seen to dive vertically from the clouds and smash into Titsey Park. It was reported that Ireland, a 22-year-old Ulsterman, had been taking part in a mock dog-fight above the clouds and lost control, or perhaps 'blacked-out' momentarily in a high 'g' manoeuvre. The following day Sydney Ireland's friend and fellow sergeant pilot, Patrick Watson-Parker died when he stalled his Spitfire as he approached Biggin Hill; the fighter dropped from the sky and crashed at Tatsfield.

---

12 July 1940

Spitfire, P9502
610 Squadron

Location:
Titsey Park
Pilot:
Sergeant
Sydney Ireland
(22) - killed

---

13 July 1940

Spitfire, R6807
610 Squadron

Location:
Skid House,
Tatsfield
Pilot:
Sergeant
P I Watson-Parker
(22) - killed

Spitfires of No.610
Squadron, early in the
summer of 1940.

The view from the gunner's postion as a group of Bf110s keep formation.

Twenty-four year old Hauptman Walter Rubensdörffer led his formation low over the English Channel towards England. Behind him twenty-one more sleek, twin engined Messerschmitt Bf110 fighter-bombers and a gaggle of eight Me109s kept formation. On his map a red pencil line ran from Calais on the French coast, across Kent and directly to Kenley. Surrey was about to receive its baptism of fire.

Rubensdörffer was confident, and he every right to be so. He had been a test pilot at the Luftwaffe's Rechlin experimental centre where he developed the concept of the fighter-bomber; an aircraft that could not only deliver bombs, but fight its way out of trouble. Barely six weeks earlier he had been given command of his own special unit, the cumbersomely named Erprobungsgruppe 210, or Test Wing 210. Now he was to test his theories under operational conditions over England. Walter was now being groomed for a top job in the victorious Luftwaffe, and he loved it. 'If I should be killed' he is reputed to have said, 'I want my ashes scattered from a plane'.

The unit had begun its battle by attacking shipping in the English Channel and off the Thames Estuary. Several ships were sunk by their bombs, but their own casualties had begun to mount.

The tall Walter Rubensdörffer is immediately recognisable on the left of this group of pilots from Erprobungsgruppe 210. The picture was taken immediately before the raid on Croydon.

It was becoming clear that the big twin-engined Bf110 could not hold its own against the more nimble Hurricanes and Spitfires that were now being met each time they set out. Within the past week they had been allotted precision targets on the English mainland; Radar stations and the fighter airfield at Manston. Yesterday they had made their second attack on Manston and the crews had seen two of their number brought down by the defending gunners.

This was the second major operation of the day for Walter Rubensdörffer and his men. The first attack had left the RAF airfield at Martlesham Heath, near Ipswich, in ruins. The route to the target had been over the sea and the pilots had successfully fended off the few defending fighters. This evening's attack was different; the target was a long way inland, he had never flown to the area before, and there would be ample time for the RAF to find them.

The formation crossed the English coast shortly after 6.30 p.m. at a speed approaching 270 miles per hour. It covered four-and-a-half miles every minute, but the target lay 65 miles away and would take at least fifteen minutes to reach.

A Messerschmitt Bf110 is 'bombed-up' before a raid. The badge showing England with a gunsight was painted on the aircraft of Erprobungsgruppe 210.

More importantly it would take another fifteen minutes to escape to the comparative safety of the Channel. Also making their way across Kent was a formation of Dornier Do17 bombers, its target was Biggin Hill. Rubensdörffer knew that the lumbering bomber formation would attract the majority of the defending fighters and, so he hoped, his faster formation would slip through unnoticed. He also knew that the fighter protection he had been promised was not with him. The flight-plan was to pass over Sevenoaks before turning the formation to port towards Kenley and then make a diving attack which would see them heading south without delay. The low evening sun was now directly ahead and a mist was beginning to form that obscured the ground and made navigation over the unfamiliar countryside difficult. A few miles further north the grey mass of London was seen spreading away as far as eye could see, the first time any of these airmen had seen the Capital of their enemy.

From a height of around 10,000 feet, Rubensdörffer picked out his target and pushed the nose of his Bf110 down into a 45 degree dive as he armed the electrically fused bombs. Horst Fiedler, the unit's Adjutant, followed and behind him came Karl-Heinz Koch, the Technical Officer, the rest of his formation followed the leading three. Streaking low over the airfield each of the Bf110 pilots released his pair of 500 kilo bombs and the eight Me109 pilots each dropped their single bomb, thirty bombs in all, onto the buildings and the landing ground – at Croydon. The

Horst Marx stands in front of a Bf110, but on this day he flew a single-engined Me109 escort fighter.

mistake was understandable, Kenley lay barely three miles away and the visibility was poor. Anyway, one airfield was a good as another. As the raiders flew over the target they opened fire with machine-guns and cannons. The anti-aircraft gunners of Croydon's defences had mistaken the raiders for Blenheims and did not open fire. Rubensdörffer pulled his aircraft up into a vertical climb, leaving a pall of dust and smoke rising behind him, and then felt it shudder under him as bullets struck into the airframe. Behind him his gunner Ludwig Kretzer opened fire at their attacker, but the gun fell silent; he had been killed. The Messerschmitt was already badly damaged and a long way from safety.

The sky filled with Hurricanes just as the bombers climbed away to the south. Low, and having traded their speed for height, the Messerschmitts had been caught at just the wrong moment. The formation immediately organized itself into a huge circle over the North Downs, with each aircraft providing protective fire for the one ahead as they gained height. The Hurricanes snapped at their heels as best they could and anti-aircraft fire found its mark. Then the formation broke. Three groups of aircraft began a head-long dash southwards towards clouds and safety, but they had lost their mutual protection.

The good people of Croydon peer over the fence as smoke rises from the airfield.

Over Redhill two Hurricane pilots chased Horst Fiedler until they saw the Messerschmitt's port engine burst into flames and the aircraft plunge into the ground with a terrific explosion. Another two Hurricanes chased their prey from the Downs, over Bletchingley and Redhill to Horley. The Bf110 gradually lost height and finally fell to earth under a hail of machine-gun fire.

In a few minutes the once disciplined formation had scattered, leaving every man to fend for himself. The pilots and gunners could only look on in disbelief and horror as they watched their comrades stagger and fall in the distance.

Helmut Ortner tried desperately to evade three Hurricanes as he fled over Kent. The port engine of his Messerschmitt was trailing a long banner of white smoke and Bernhard Lohmann was either dead or unconscious in the cockpit behind him. Finally, Ortner was forced to bale out over Ightham and leave his gunner to go down with the aircraft. Alfred Habisch's aircraft was shaking badly after it had been damaged in the circle. Unmolested by fighters he struggled to keep his aircraft in the air until he was forced to put it down safely near Hawkhurst and surrender to the Home Guard.

The port engine of Karl-Heinz Koch's Messerschmitt had been hit while he circled over the Downs, but he limped to the south coast before more Hurricanes attacked and forced him crash land near Hastings.

One of the single engine Me109s was being flown by Horst Marx. After the attack he had seen a damaged Bf110 heading away and attempted to protect it from further attacks. The pilot had radioed that he was wounded and his gunner was already dead, that pilot was none other than his commanding officer, Walter Rubensdörffer. Marx turned to head off an attack, but bullets from a Hurricane's

Shelters in the surrounding area were destroyed by stray bombs.

guns damaged his engine and Marx was forced to take to his parachute over Frant. His charge limped on towards Tunbridge Wells. Now alone in a damaged aircraft and with no gunner to protect him from a rear attack, Rubensdörffer was easy prey. Another Hurricane came into view in the Messerschmitt's mirror and slowly came closer until it could open fire. One of the engines burst into flames and he lost control. Walter Rubensdörffer went down in a streak of flames.

Of the twenty-two Bf110s that attacked Croydon six had been shot down, two more returned to Calais with serious damage and others sustained minor bullet holes. Erprobungsgruppe 210 had lost thirteen men including its commanding officer, its adjutant and its technical officer, but it would soon be back.

On the ground at Croydon the choking dust settled and the acrid smoke from burning buildings and equipment cleared to reveal a scene, the horror of which was unimaginable to all but those who had survived the trenches of the First War. Every one of the be-suited gentlemen from the Board of Management of the once German owned NSF factory lay dead. They had been holding a meeting at the very moment of the attack. The Redwing Aircraft factory was destroyed and 'C' Hangar used by Rollason's was set alight and the training aircraft in it destroyed. The armoury received a direct hit and the Officer's Mess was destroyed by the blast from a near miss. The terminal buildings and 'A' and 'D' Hangars were damaged. Outside the airfield the factories of Bourjois Scent, Mullard and Phillips were damaged. Bombs missing their target exploded in Crowley Crescent, Coldharbour Way, Foss Avenue and Waddon Way on the neighbouring Waddon estate. Delayed action bombs continued to explode into the evening, hindering efforts to recover the injured from collapsed buildings. Eventually the bodies of sixty-two civilians were found, 192 more had been injured to varying degrees. Surprisingly, only six servicemen had been killed, five from No. 111 Squadron and one from the Station Headquarters. Fifteen minutes after the attack the air raid sirens sounded. Significantly the attack on Croydon, classified as Greater London, directly contravened Hitler's orders not to attack London. The air war had just escalated by another degree.

On Croydon airfield itself, ground crew and staff of No. 111 Squadron awaited the return of the nine Hurricane pilots who had scrambled only minutes before the bombing. Squadron Leader John Thompson had been ordered to take his men to the west of the airfield and was still climbing when he saw the bombers diving at the airfield from the opposite side. One by one all nine pilots returned safely, the canvas patches that sealed the eight machine-gun

The grave of Aircraftman Adams, killed on the ground during the raid.

ports in their wings blasted away. The squadron's intelligence officer collected their combat reports to submit to Fighter Command HQ. Thompson had attacked the leading twin-engined Messerschmitt as it climbed vertically after its bombing run - Rubensdörffer. Sergeant Dymond reported that his victim had crashed at Redhill after a Biggin Hill Hurricane had joined in. Flight Lieutenant Connors and another pilot brought down the aircraft that fell near Horley. Sergeants Craig and Wallace attacked the enemy, but could not confirm they had crashed.

A similar scene was being repeated at Biggin Hill, to where the pilots of No. 32 Squadron returned. Sergeant Pearce claimed that he shared the Messerschmitt at Redhill with Sergeant Dymond. Flight Lieutenant Michael Crossley led his Red Section and with his numbers two and three brought down the aircraft at Ightham.

From the Training Flight, Flight Lieutenant Humphrey Russell contributed to the aircraft down at Hastings, and Pilot Officer 'Polly' Flinders brought down the single Me109.

But it was Pilot Officer Duckenfield, of No.501 Squadron returning from a different patrol, who chanced upon Rubensdörffer's already damaged machine and administered the coup de gras.

The original grave markers of the three Bf110 crewmen at Burstow (St Bartholomews) Churchyard. The graves were marked as 'Unknown German Airmen' but were correctly identified after the war and moved to the central German military cemetery at Cannock Chase.

CRASH INVESTIGATION

Of the seven aircraft that crashed during this raid, two fell in the county of Surrey, at Redhill and Horley.

15 August 1940

Messerschmitt Bf110C-6
S9+TH, 1/Eprg 210
Location:
**Broadbridge Farm, Smallfield,
near Horley**

Time: 18.50 hours

Crew:
**Leutnant Erich Beudel (20) - killed,
Obergefreiter Otto Jordan (19) - killed**

Shot down by Flight Lieutenant Connors, possibly with Sergeant Wallace, both of No. 111 Squadron.

Eighteen-year-old Glen Cooper of Suconnex Farm was cutting wood brought from plum trees when he first saw the aircraft appear from the north, with RAF fighters in pursuit. The aircraft flew over Weather Hill and Green Farm, weaving to avoid the fighters. After more gunfire the Messerschmitt turned back towards Smallfield and flew slowly over him. A Hurricane then opened fire, sending streams of spent cartridge cases spilling from its eight guns.

Mr Cooper recalled to historian Dennis Knight many years later: "The aircraft seemed to break up, or start to, bits came off, a puff of oily smoke, the figure of a man appeared as one of the crew jumped."

The aircraft then fell to the ground a few fields away from where Glen and his friend Mr Fisher stood. Both men ran towards where the aircraft fell. A path led along a hedgerow towards the crash and it was along this that Glen raced, until he came across the body of an airman. The figure was lying on his back. He was dressed in grey denim overalls and wore a Mae West, brown leather flying boots and a brown leather helmet. His facial features were distorted and his head was smashed from impact with the ground. One leg was badly fractured and hardly joined to the body.

Across the hedge the wreckage of the Messerschmitt was strewn. Glen and his younger brother John took the helmet and one flying boot as souvenirs. A signal pistol tempted them, but the elder Mr Fisher dissuaded them from taking the firearm. The fighter that had shot it down then roared over the scene and climbed away.

More people were now arriving in search of their own souvenirs; troops and police were having difficulty sealing off the area.

Further down Broadfield Lane the body of a second German airman was found lying at the foot of tall pine trees. The bodies were laid to rest in Burstow (St Bartholomews) Churchyard and marked as 'Unknown German Airmen'. They were moved after the war to the central German military cemetery at Cannock Chase where they were correctly identified.

The day after the crash, RAF intelligence officers inspected the wreckage and discovered a 30mm cannon that had been mounted beneath the fuselage for attacking ground targets. This turned out to be a most unusual weapon. It was only fitted to a handful of Bf110s and it was the only one ever to be found in Britain.

Today a continuous stream of airliners pass over the crash site as it lies directly under the flight path to Gatwick Airport.

---

15 August 1940

Messerschmitt Bf110D
W.Nr.3374, S9+BB, Stab/Eprg 210

Time: 18.50 Hours

Crew:
Oberleutnant Horst Fiedler (27) - killed
Unteroffizier Johann Werner - prisoner

Location:
Redhill Airfield

Shot down by Sergeant William Dymond of No.111 Squadron and Sergeant Pearce of No. 32 Squadron.

POLICE REPORT:

"I was on enquiries in Nutfield when an air battle took place in a north-north-easterly direction (Croydon). About 7.00 p.m. I observed an aircraft apparently out of control coming down in spirals from a height of approximately 5,000 feet in the direction of Redhill Aerodrome. In the same section of sky a parachute was descending."

PC 52 E. Beeney

PC Beeney then went to the crash site and found the body of Horst Fiedler in the burnt-out wreckage. Johann Werner, the gunner / wireless operator, bailed out and landed near Merstham where he was captured by men of the 3rd Canadian Infantry Brigade.

The West Nova Scotia Regiment recorded:

"The Company Commander's conference was badly disorganised when an aerial dogfight started overhead. Actually orders called for a cessation of all movements around the O.P. area, but everyone forgot orders in their excitement over the dogfight. A flight of British fighters had intercepted a flight of twelve German bombers. This was something new to most of those present who were viewing real war and hearing the rattle of machine-gun fire in earnest for the first time.

"Doubtless there were few who realised or thought of the grimness of the 'show' that they were thoroughly enjoying. The British anti-aircraft fire broke up the German formation and gave the fighters their opportunity, which they made use of to the excitement and enjoyment of the group of officers and men gathered to receive orders for tomorrow's war week.

"In very short order five or six of the German bombers were knocked off by the RAF and one bomber, trailing smoke from the tail, passed over our O.P. Two of the crew baled out, one parachute did not function, the other did and drifted with its occupant in the direction of the O.P. *

"When it was seen that the German was going to land near us there was much loading of rifle and fixing of bayonets and drawing of revolvers, accompanied by threats of what would befall the enemy when he landed.

"Finally he did drop down a short distance from the O.P. and landed in a group of men large enough to have captured a whole battalion. Despite the threats that had been made our men did not 'polish off' the German. Quite the contrary, within a few minutes they had his wounds, of which there were several, bandaged with their field dressings and some were offering him smokes. The parachute disappeared in remarkably short order having been cut into small pieces for souvenirs. The prisoner was hustled into our ambulance and his wounds were properly dressed, after which he was taken under guard to Divisional HQ where he was handed to the Intelligence Officer and a receipt obtained for him. This is our first prisoner and is in fact the first prisoner taken by the 1ˢᵗ Canadian Division."

The wreck of Horst Fiedler's Bf110 at Redhill.

*Clearly the Canadian correspondent witnessed the Redhill crash, but confused the airmen who fell without a parachute with the crash at Horley a couple of miles further south.

18TH AUGUST 1940

Sunday 18th August was another hard fought day of the battle and, by some measures, the hardest day for the RAF. During the day the Luftwaffe launched three major set-piece attacks against southern England; 100 German fighters and bombers 50 aircraft of Fighter Command were lost or damaged.

Thomas Prickman, the thirty-eight year old Wing Commander and Station Commander of RAF Kenley, was on duty in the single story brick-built Sector Operations building. Protected by high blast walls he and his staff watched the markers, or 'plots', being placed on the operations table by the WAAFs. The system of radio detection stations around the coast and Observer Corps posts was working well. All this information was being gathered at the 11 Group operations room at Uxbridge, from where messages were passed by telephone to Kenley. Just after 1 o'clock it was becoming clear to Prickman that another raid was developing over Kent and once again heading towards the 11 Group airfields of Kenley, Croydon and Biggin Hill.

The Spitfires of No. 64 Squadron and Hurricanes of No. 615 Squadron had already left Kenley to join No. 32 and 610 Squadrons from Biggin Hill. The Fighter Control Officer, Squadron Leader Norman, was attempting to get them into a position to intercept the steadily approaching raid at around 20,000 feet. To be in

Dornier Do17s, known as 'flying pencils' to the British.

A high altitude photo of Kenley showing the burning buildings immediately after the attack.

an advantageous position, Norman had to get his fighters above the enemy, almost five miles high.

A WAAF then began to move a new plot over the table, pushing the 'hostile' marker north of Burgess Hill and along the line of the Brighton to London railway line. More reports from the Observer Corps clarified the situation, nine bombers at zero feet – heading north. Only one conclusion could be reached; *both* forces were heading for the airfields!

Hurriedly, Prickman issued the instruction to get every airworthy machine into the air; anything not ready for combat should head north and out of trouble, the Hurricanes of Treble-One Squadron should scramble from Croydon and go south to meet the low-level raid now streaking over the roof tops of Bletchingley. In a few minutes it would be clear who was going to 'clobbered' today.

By twenty-past one on a sunny Sunday afternoon the stage had been set and all the players were in place for a deadly aerial ballet. In the next five minutes, less time than it takes to read this account, the biggest single air battle fought over Surrey would take place.

THE PLAYERS:

HIGH-LEVEL RAID

Between and four and five miles above east Surrey the high-level German force was heading from Sevenoaks to Kenley. There were twenty-seven Dornier Do17s and twelve Junkers Ju88s of the bomber unit Kampfgeshwader 76 accompanied by twenty Messerschmitt Bf110 and up to sixty Me109 fighters flying over them. On their way to meet them head-on were the Hurricanes and Spitfires from Kenley and Biggin Hill.

LOW-LEVEL RAID

At tree-top height over Bletchingley, flying north to Kenley, were the nine Dorniers of the specialist low-level attack unit 9 Staffel, Kampfgeshwader 76 (9./KG76). Heading south from Croydon were the Hurricanes of No. 111 Squadron, over Kenley at around 3,000 feet.

HIGH-LEVEL RAID

Squadron Leader Kayll was leading the Hurricanes of 615 (County of Surrey) Squadron in a climb to 25,000 feet, and had been ordered to head north. This put them in a perilous position with the sun behind and unable to see an approaching enemy on their tail against the glare. Part of the formation then broke away and headed towards the Sevenoaks and Edenbridge area, the remainder carried on over the Sutton area, keeping a look-out for the fighter escort as best as they could.

As feared, the Messerschmitts of Jagdgeschwader 3 had manoeuvred themselves up-sun of the Hurricanes into a perfect position from which to 'bounce' them; the tactic worked perfectly. The Hurricane pilots, dazzled by the sun, could not see their attackers and were caught unawares. 'Dutch' Hugo saw Sergeant Walley go down on fire away to his starboard, then his own Hurricane was hit and he went spinning down. Pilot Officer Looker went into a spin after his aircraft was damaged.

10,000 feet below, the twelve Hurricane pilots of No. 32 Squadron held steady for a head-on attack on the Dorniers. The Bf110 escort then appeared and 'B' Flight broke away to head them off, leaving 'A' Flight to break-up the formation. Pilot Officer Alan Eckford focused on the lead bomber and opened fire at a

'Dutch' Hugo, who was shot down during this engagement. See his account opposite.

DUTCH HUGO'S ACCOUNT

Hugo injured the day before, had both legs bandaged. Hurricane KW-J was shining like a new pin and ready for operations.

Sunday, August l8th, dawned bright and clear - how often we prayed for bad weather to allow us to catch up on our sleep and rest - and the Squadron was on readiness early.

During the morning we were kept informed of enemy activity and expected orders to scramble any minute. KW-J was lined up with the Squadron just off the perimeter track.

I had my parachute in the seat, my helmet plugged in to the oxygen and RT and hung over the reflector sight. I was by no means small and I used this method to speed up my 'scramble' time, rather than the more normal one of having the parachute on the wing, putting it on and then climbing into the cockpit.

About half-past twelve we were scrambled and within minutes the squadron was making height to the south-southeast with the CO leading 'B' Flight and myself flying No.3 in Red Section of 'A' Flight. Our instructions were to intercept bombers approaching the South Coast, but soon this was changed and we were ordered to climb to 25,000 feet on a northerly course to intercept enemy fighters. This put the sun in the worst possible tactical position, practically dead astern, and the squadron opened formation with Elmer Gaunce leading 'A' Flight over to port and slightly above 'B' Flight.

Enemy fighters were reported in the vicinity but we saw nothing until we were nearly at 25,000 feet when vapour trails appeared high to starboard. By this time I was feeling distinctly unhappy; my legs were swollen, ached savagely, and the bandages were much too tight, restricting circulation and making my feet cold.

In addition I realised that with the sun behind us and enemy fighters above we were sitting targets. I literally and figuratively had 'cold feet'.

Suddenly, almost magically, an Me109E appeared behind Sergeant Walley, flying No. 2 in Green Section on the extreme starboard. I yelled a warning over the R/T and turned sharply to starboard to engage the enemy fighter, but already it was too late. Sergeant Walley's machine burst into flames and before I had more than started to turn all hell broke loose.

There was a blinding flash and a deafening explosion in the left side of the cockpit somewhere behind the instrument panel, my left leg received a numbing, sickening, blow and a sheet of high octane petrol shot back into the cockpit from the main tank. My stricken Hurricane flicked over into a spin and must have been hit half a dozen times while doing so, as the sledgehammer cracks of cannon and machine-gun strikes went on for what seemed ages.

Without any conscious effort I had turned off the fuel, put the airscrew into fine pitch and opened the throttle wide before the spin had really started, to use up the fuel in the carburetor as soon as possible and decrease the risk of fire - the dreadful bogey of all pilots.

Petrol was gushing into the cockpit and I was soaked through to the skin, but I dared not open the cockpit hood to bale out as the flaming exhaust stubs were glowing right in front of the cockpit and one spark would have turned everything into a blazing inferno.

Finally the engine coughed, spluttered and ceased firing; I put the airscrew into coarse pitch and switched off the ignition. The airscrew slowed down until it was just flicking over lazily in the slipstream and I knew the immediate danger of fire was over.

A sigh of relief and a prayer of thankfulness seemed to be in order as I slowly pulled out of the spin, but in any case both were rather premature - no sooner had the sky and earth returned to their proper places than there was a most colossal bang behind me and the now familiar sound of cannon strikes. I must have got the biggest fright of my life I knew I was completely incapable of movement as a particularly vicious looking Me109E with a yellow nose snarled about twenty feet past my starboard wing, the venomous crackle of his Daimler-Benz engine clearly audible.

Round he came for another attack and although I did everything I could think of, gliding without power has its limitations and next moment earth and sky seemed to explode into crimson flame as I received the most almighty blow on the side of the head.

I came to, feeling sick and shaken, to find the aircraft spinning comfortably. Through a red haze I could see that I was still some 10,000 feet up, so took stock of the situation. My head was aching savagely and the right side of my face felt numb. When I touched it I found a jagged gash from the corner of my right jaw to my chin and another shorter cut on the outside of my right eyebrow.

The microphone and oxygen mask had been torn off my helmet and were draped by their leads over my right forearm; the microphone had a bullet hole through it.

The cockpit appeared to have lots more ventilation in it than normally and was filled with a fine red spray. It took me some time to realise that blood was pouring down over my chest and was being whipped by the wind into a spray. The cockpit hood was getting covered inside with a mixture of petrol and blood and was difficult to see through, so I slid it back and gulped in huge lungfuls of clean air.

I must have corrected the spin automatically, because next moment the 109 was banking around getting set for another attack, but I decided that being a sitting target had no attraction and that baling out was indicated. A quick half roll left me hanging upside-down in the safety harness, so I pulled the locking pin out, expecting to fall cleanly clear of the machine.

To my consternation I fell only about twelve inches - just sufficient to project my head, arms and shoulders into the solid blast of the slipstream, which immediately pinned those parts firmly against the hood and the fuselage, leaving about three quarters of my body in the cockpit.

Before I could cope with the unexpected situation my Hurricane - thoroughbred that it was - solved the problem by diving through the second half of a loop.

The increase of the slipstream when going vertically down before levelling out felt as if I was going to pull my head right off and the final pull out, when gravity forced me back into the cockpit, seemed to take all the skin and flesh off my back and shoulders. However, at the end of the unorthodox manoeuvre I was back in the cockpit, rather puzzled but once more in control.

By this time I was running out of altitude and the fat sausage shapes of the London balloon barrage seemed uncomfortably close. The pest of a 109 appeared on the scene again, but fortunately made a mess of his next attack, but even so the last 4,000 feet was hectic to say the least.

In between watching this persistent blighter, finding the safety straps to strap in with for the now inevitable crash landing, looking for a suitable field to come down in and avoiding two more attacks, I was as busy as a one-armed one-man bandsman with a flea in his pants.

During this time I also found out why my machine seemed to have such a strong attachment (literally) for me; when hurriedly strapping on my parachute before take-off I had accidentally put the right hand leg strap around the lever used to lower and raise the pilot's seat, thus firmly strapping myself to the machine.

The field I had chosen to crash-land in was coming up fast and with a final wild side-slip and a violent skid to put my unwelcome companion off I came in over the trees which almost surrounded it and started to flatten out. The speed was far too great and as it dropped off I realised that the amount of damage to my tailplane and elevators was so much that I couldn't get the tail down to the stalling position.

The touch-down was very fast but surprisingly gentle - hunks of turf flew all over the place and chunks of splintered airscrew blades whizzed past the cockpit and I decided, again very prematurely, that I was down.

Again I undid the safety harness and started to stand up, only to be thrown violently forward as the machine decelerated and the radiator dug a long furrow in the field before being torn off. The nose of the machine dug in and the tail reared up, my chest was smashed against the curving edge of the windscreen and the partnership of pilot and Hurricane finished up in an untidy heap with me thrown half out of the cockpit (fortunately I had jettisoned a panel on the starboard side at the last moment, because the attached leg strap of the parachute sandwiched me neatly into the gap).

Grateful as I was to the faithful KW-J for bringing me safely back to terra-firma, I lost no time in scrambling clear of her in case fire started.

From about twenty yards away I surveyed the wreck of what had been a shining brand new Hurricane less than an hour ego.

The airscrew blades were splintered off close to the spinner; there was a gaping hole that exposed the tank on the port side, in front of the cockpit; the rear fuselage and tail seemed to be completely stripped of fabric and the radiator was lying a hundred yards away in a deep furrow the aircraft had dug.

This proved to be my last look - next moment I was in the clutches of half a dozen cheerful and eager ambulance men who soon had me wrapped up in bandages till I could hardly breathe, dumped me on a stretcher and trotted off to where their ambulance was parked in the wood a few hundred yards away.

Soon afterwards I was on the operating table of the War Emergency Hospital, Orpington, where the gashes on my face were sewn up and a machine-gun bullet removed from my left leg. The uninhibited and colourful language of the New Zealand surgeon as he stitched, snipped and probed for the bullets is the only part of this experience that gave me any pleasure.

In the ward eventually I found out from Squadron Leader Gleave, who had been shot down and cruelly burnt, and 'Fluid', an Army Major who had his right leg more or less blown off at Dunkirk, that this surgeon was a known character, and their efforts to stimulate his vocabulary invariably resulted in our two favourite nurses, Blossom and Norrie, hastily departing with flaming cheeks.

Next day I rang up the Squadron Adjutant Wally Stern to try and get me out of hospital. After a long delay I eventually spoke to him; he sounded tired and depressed, so unlike the lively Adj to whom everybody always took their troubles.

I asked him to get Doc to hustle over the blood-wagon and bail me out of hospital. There was a long pause, so long that I thought he had not heard me, then he quietly told me that he had just come back from Whyteleafe cemetery - surely the most beautiful of all churchyards - where they had laid Doc to rest. He had been killed instantly in a raid on Kenley the day before.

And so finished all too many of those fine youngsters, the cream of manhood from England and the British Isles, from Canada, Australia, New Zealand, South Africa and Rhodesia, from France, Poland. Czechoslovakia, Holland, Belgium, Denmark, and Norway, and from many other countries, including the U.S.A., The Argentine, Lithuania, and even, incredibly, Russia, (wearing the shoulder flashes of Canada). Only History will prove whether their supreme sacrifice was justified, and to history the "Battle of Britain" will revert.

range of half-a-mile, just over three seconds when the two aircraft were closing at eight miles a minute! He flashed through the enemy formation and emerged safely behind to see one of the Dorniers stagger upwards, then lazily turn over and begin to spin the four miles down to earth.

The Bf110s joined combat with No. 32 Squadron and 'Humph' Russell baled out. Squadron Leader MacDonell now led his twelve Spitfires of No. 64 Squadron into the battle, joining the remnants of Nos. 615 and 32 Squadrons; at least six of these pilots set about a single Ju88 that finally blew up over Ide Hill. 'Elmer' Gaunce of 615 Squadron, who had broken away from the squadron in the climb, jumped out of blazing machine over Edenbridge.

The high level raid had been broken up and dispersed, the bombs falling over north-east Surrey and Croydon.

LOW LEVEL

Hauptmann Joachim Roth was precisely on time and route when he crested the North Downs. 9./KG76, uniquely among bomber crews, had been issued with steel helmets to protect themselves from shrapnel and the Dorniers each had a 20mm cannon to fire at targets on the ground. According to the briefing Kenley airfield should have been bombed by the high force just minutes before, clearing the way for his low-level run over the target. Far from taking cover, the airfield's defences were waiting for them.

In addition to the Bofors and Lewis guns, Kenley had been equipped with an unusual device designed for the very purpose of bringing down low-level raiders. The rocket powered 'Parachute and Cable' equipment would fire a curtain of steel ropes into the air, trailing parachutes to literally drag aircraft from the sky.

Roth and his men came racing over the southern boundary of the airfield, line abreast and as low as they dare, with Connors in his Hurricane right on their tails.

Anti aircraft guns were sited around Kenley ready to repel any attack.

Every gun opened fire. Within seconds every bomber in the formation was hit. Bombs exploded. Three hangars collapsed and other buildings shook. Eight Hurricanes were destroyed and nine men killed. Men and women surprised by the attack dived into shelters and trenches.

On the far side of the airfield Aircraftman Roberts held his nerve

in the path of the approaching Dorniers. The rockets rose into the air, trailing their cables and parachutes in the smoke behind them. A bomber struck a cable, swung wildly, then recovered control. A second bomber, already on fire, then hit a cable that ensnared it. The parachutes at either end of the cable opened and dragged the struggling aircraft out of the sky; it exploded with a terrific roar only yards away from the rocket launchers. Two of the Hurricanes had also been hit in the confusion;

Stanley Connors was seen chasing the leading bomber, but his Hurricane fell not far from the airfield. Pilot Officer Simpson headed west and put his damaged machine down safely on a golf course.

The surviving bombers limped away with smoking engines and wounded or dying crew, with the pilots of 111 Squadron in pursuit.

In the lead bomber Rudolf Lamberty was at the controls, his commanding officer Joachim Roth sitting next to him. The left wing and engine of the Dornier were already in flames, but still Hurricanes chased the crippled machine, the bullets hitting it repeatedly. The aircraft staggered on westward into Kent, where it crash-landed in a field at Leaves Green.

Nineteen-year-old Harry Newton was on the tail of the Dornier flown by Günther Unger that had already lost its right engine. Over Woldingham the two aircraft exchanged fire, but Newton's Hurricane came off worse and caught fire; he baled out with seconds to spare.

Of the seven bombers that escaped, two were so badly damaged that the pilots were forced to land in the sea near the French coast, two more crash landed in French fields and the others managed to land at airfields in France.

Dennis Knight's analysis of the Kenley raid.
(Courtesy of Larry Hickey).

I/KG 76 approching to bomb from high altitude

9 Staffel KG 76 make low–level attack on Kenley Fighter Station 18th August 1940.

Fw Stephani force-landed Calais

Flintfield

Whytelaafe Road

Operations block

Officer's Mess

Oblt Maqin shot Ofw Illg takes control

Uffz Schumacher Ditched in Channel

615 Sqn. dispersal aera

Fw Raab F1+LT returned damaged

Oblt Lamberty Hpt Roth F1+DT crashed in Kent

F1+

Sunneycroft

Oblt Ahrends Oberst Somm

Sgt Newton

F/L Connors leading a section III Sqn Hurricanes

Sgt Deacon

Caterham Guard's Depot

Salmons Lane   Grove Ho WAAF's Barrack Blocks   Guard Room

Sergeant's   Hullhurst
Mess

Medical Centre
Shelters hit

Headquarters

Building

P/O Loft takes-off
during bombing

Fuel store

Shooting range

Uffz Maassen
returned

Uffz Unger
Ditched in Channel

parachute & cable screen   Fw Reichel
                            F I + CT
                            crash-landed in France

Fuel tanker
explodes

64 Sqn dispersal hern

Dennis Knight.

Golf Road   The Crest Demolished

29

Still in the air as the raiders retreated were the Hurricane pilots, unfortunately the shocked gunners on the airfields were still on a state of high alert. Pilot Officer Looker of No. 615 Squadron, trying to land at Croydon after engaging the high level raid, was fired at just as he came in to land. His aircraft was seriously damaged as it skidded across the grass, but he escaped with his life.

Harry Deacon of No. 111 Squadron was nursing his damaged aircraft back to Croydon and was also coping with the pain from a leg that had been injured by return fire. He was flying at around 250 feet over near Kenley when the gunners opened fire at him and hit the Hurricane's right wing. Fortunately he had just enough time to get out before his fighter dived into a wood and exploded.

The Kenley raid left two German bombers and six RAF Hurricanes wrecked in the Surrey landscape.

---

18 August 1940

Hurricane, R4187	**Time: 13.30**
111 Squadron	Pilot:
Location:	**Flight Lieutenant Stanley Dudley Pierce**
Near Leaves Green	**Connors (28) - killed**

STANLEY CONNORS

Stanley Connors was born in Calcutta, in 1912 and spent his early years in India. He was at first rejected by the RAF in 1931 due to a heart condition, but was accepted when he re-applied in 1935. In 1937 he obtained a short service commission for five years as a pilot officer in the Auxiliary Air Force and began his training as a fighter pilot.

He went to France with No. 111 Squadron and won the DFC for efforts against the Luftwaffe. During the Battle of Britain he was based at Croydon and continued his distinguished career as a fighter pilot with a total of twelve enemy aircraft destroyed to his credit; he was one of the highest scoring pilots of the time. He left his wife, Marjorie and yet-to-be born daughter Mercedes. He is buried North Berwick Cemetery, East Lothian.

FLIGHT LIEUTENANT CONNORS VICTORY CLAIMS:

18 May	Ju88	31 July	Ju88 probable
18 May	Me109	11 August	Me109
19 May	3 x He111, 1 x Ju88	15 August	Ju88
31 May	Me109	15 August	Bf110
2 June	He111	15 August	Ju88 damaged
7 June	Me109	15 August	Bf110 damaged
19 July	Me109	16 August	Do17 probable
25 July	Me109 damaged	18 August	Do17 probable

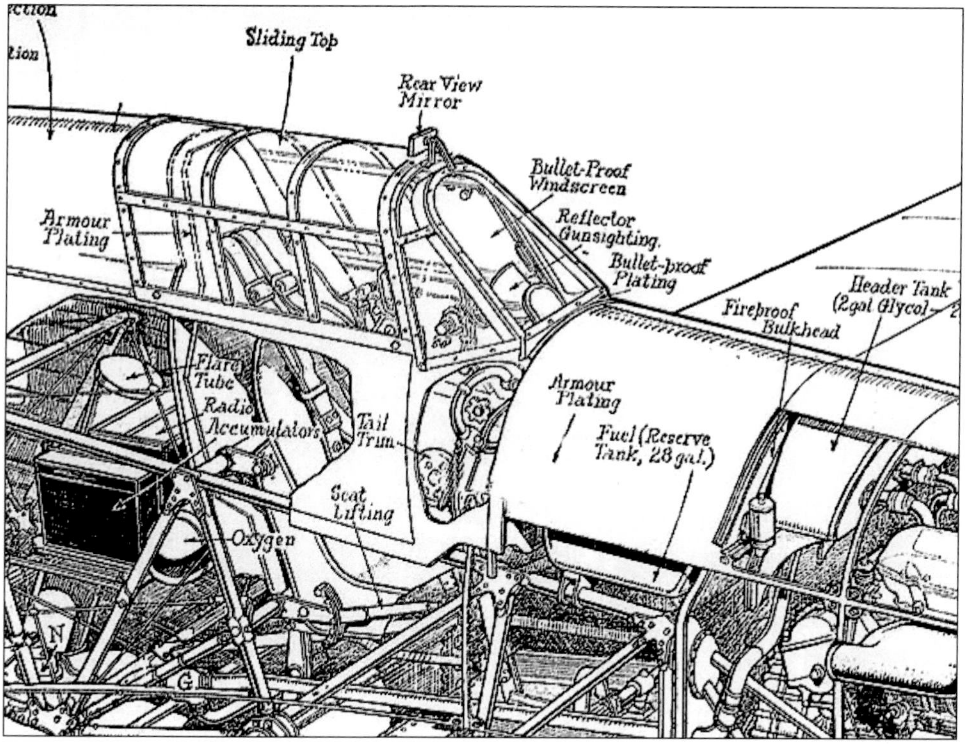
Sliding Top
Rear View Mirror
Bullet-Proof Windscreen
Reflector Gunsighting.
Bullet-proof Plating
Header Tank (2gal Glycol)
Fireproof Bulkhead
Armour Plating
Flare Tube
Radio
Accumulators
Tail Trim
Armour Plating
Fuel (Reserve Tank, 28 gal.)
Seat Lifting
Oxygen

Many fighter pilots suffered terrible burns when they were shot down. This illustration of a Hurricane shows the 28 gallon fuel tank just inches in front of the pilot; any bullet hole in this would spray petrol straight into the cockpit.

CRASH INVESTIGATION

For many years it was believed that Stanley Connors' Hurricane had crashed in the grounds of a large house known as 'The Oaks' at Wallington, but this has recently been proved untrue. An aircraft did fall at 'The Oaks', but this was a Spitfire that crashed in 1941.

Stanley Connors had taken his Hurricane down into the formation of Dorniers as they made their attack on Kenley airfield. His aircraft was hit by return fire from the bombers, or anti-aircraft fire, or perhaps both, but he was seen to turn to starboard and head east, over Kenley Valley.

Very low and still doggedly in pursuit of the bombers, observers on the ground saw that his Hurricane was on fire. In a burning aircraft and at such a low level Connors must have known that he had no chance of survival.

As many other fighter pilots found, any fire turned the cockpit into furnace fuelled by high octane petrol from the tank immediately in front to them; Connors had no time to climb to a height where he could bale out. His burning aircraft was seen to strike the ground a glancing blow at high speed. It broke up on impact, the engine breaking away and travelling on further. Connors' partly burnt body was thrown from the wreck.

18 August 1940

Hurricane, P3399
111 Squadron
Location:
Woodcote Park Golf Course, Epsom

Time: 13.30
Pilot:
Pilot Officer Peter James Simpson (21)
safe

Peter Simpson attacked the Dorniers over Kenley behind Stanley Connors. His Hurricane was hit by return fire from the bombers as he broke away and his rudder and aileron controls were damaged.

A shell splinter had injured a foot and he decided to make a wheels-up landing on the RAC golf course that appeared in front of him.

"I jumped down off the wing, landed on the foot with a splinter in it and cried out with pain. At that moment other people approached, one of who said he was a doctor. He sat me down, took my shoe and sock off, and pulled out one of the splinters. My foot was all numb, with blood pouring out; I thought the whole foot was going to have to come off!"

The members helped their honoured guest to the clubhouse where was offered lunch and brandy, before being driven back to Croydon.

Recently, the Royal Automobile Club commissioned artist Mark Postlethwaite to produce a painting of the incident that now hangs on the clubhouse wall.

Mark Postlethwaite's painting of Simpson's Hurricane now hangs on the wall of the clubhouse in the background.

18 August 1940

Hurricane, P3943
111 Squadron
Location:
Botley Hill, east of Woldingham

Time: 13.30
Pilot:
**Sergeant Harry Snow Newton (20)
injured**

Harry Newton was a frequent visitor to the shows held at Kenley in the 1980s.

The events surrounding this particular event are among the most fully documented of the Battle of Britain, thanks to the research done by Dr. Alfred Price for his book, 'The Hardest Day'. Harry Newton was shot down by return fire from Franz Bergmann, gunner in the Dornier of Günther Unger that had just taken part in the low level strike on Kenley. The pilots met again in 1978.

Researcher Peter Foote met Harry at Kenley on 16 August 1987 and recorded his description of the day:

The crash site of Harry Newton's Hurricane.

"I had just taken off from Croydon with 85 gallons of fuel, 35 in each wing tank and 15 in the tank ahead of the cockpit. It was return fire from a Do17 that hit me. When I looked down there was a candle-like flame at the Kigas primer, but since it wasn't in use I thought it was not seriously affecting the performance

of the aircraft. At this point I was doing about 300 mph at 150 feet, so had to think and take some drastic action.

Because the engine was still performing I decided to climb. I slid back the hood because of the fire, there was a whoosh of air and out went my maps and all the dirt off the floor.

As I climbed I got up out of the seat and on to the slid back hood and was riding the aircraft like a jockey. I waited for a bang; if it came, so be it, but it didn't. At 700 feet the engine died. With my right hand on the ripcord handle I stuck my right foot into the flames to boot the stick to the right and roll, so that I would go out left. At the moment I let go I pulled the ripcord and just missed the tail.

The flames went through three pairs of gloves on my right hand. I came down in the same field as the aircraft had crashed.

Soldiers with fixed bayonets came after me and I had to make it clear that I was on their side.

I rolled up my parachute and considered I had made a first class job of the descent. My shoes had come off because the laces had burnt through!

A young woman came up to me, but fainted. "What's up with her?" I asked, the sight of my burnt face had shocked her.

Three doctors were called from the local golf course to attend, one to my face, one to my hand and the third to my right shin. Presently a lady in a canvas covered pickup-cum ambulance arrived; she was delighted with her first 'real' casualty and took me to Oxted Hospital.

It was about 1.30 when I landed and 6 o'clock when I came round from the operations. I was promptly sick, bring up my dinner – I'd had three sweets that day. The fingers of my hand were 'pinned out' on a board that extended to my elbow. The burns were now starting to hurt. They put tannic acid and dressings on my hands, olive oil on my face and an ordinary dressing on my right shin.

Four months later I was back on the squadron, just as it was posted to Malta. I was left behind and sent to the Isle of Man to fly Ansons as an instructor."

---

18 August 1940

Hurricane, N2340   **Time: 13.30**
111 Squadron   Pilot:
Location: **Sergeant Albert Harry Deacon**
Henley Wood, Chelsham   **injured**

Harry Deacon

Harry Deacon had been a pilot in the pre-war RAF and flew with 85 Squadron during the Battle of France when he shot down several enemy aircraft. He returned to England with his squadron and moved to 111 Squadron on 17 August; less than 24 hours later he was shot down. Harry finished the war as a flying instructor in South Africa.

34

Sergeant Deacon with his pre-war biplane fighter.

After being wounded in a leg by enemy fire from the low level Dorniers of 9./KG76 Harry Deacon had the misfortune to be hit by anti-aircraft fire near Kenley. It is reported that the right outer section of the wing 'folded up' and the aircraft rolled over at a height of just 250 feet. Fortunately the pilot's parachute had time to deploy and he escaped further injury. The Hurricane struck the ground on the northern edge of Henley Wood, not far south of the Chelsham Road, and caught fire. Harry landed near to The Harrow pub.

---

18 August 1940

Hurricane, L1592, KW-Z
615 Squadron
Location:
Croydon Airfield

Time: 13.30
Pilot:
Pilot Officer David John Looker
injured

David Looker had been educated at Eton and had been a member of the British four-man bobsleigh team that won the 1937 and 1938 World Championships.

In May 1940 he attacked an Hs126, but was then himself shot down and injured. On 18 August he had been in combat during the high level engagement that had seen Peter Walley shot down. After sustaining damage from Me109s in the engagement he put his aircraft into a violent spin in order to convince his assailants that he been shot down. Recovering from his spin at around 4,000 feet, he had been on the point of baling out and had undone his harness when he noticed Croydon airfield below and changed his mind, deciding instead to put down on the field that he had flown from before the war.

As he approached over the Purley Way with his wheels down the trigger-happy gunners opened up, but by then he had no option but to land straight ahead. The Hurricane landed heavily and nose-down, causing it to nose over. The aircraft was badly damaged and Looker suffered concussion when he was thrown against the gun sight and instrument panel, which put him in hospital for a month.

He later rejoined the squadron and was then posted as an instructor to Canada. The Hurricane was repaired and survived the war.

As L1592 was one of the very first Hurricanes to be built it was kept after the war and is now on display at the Science Museum in London.

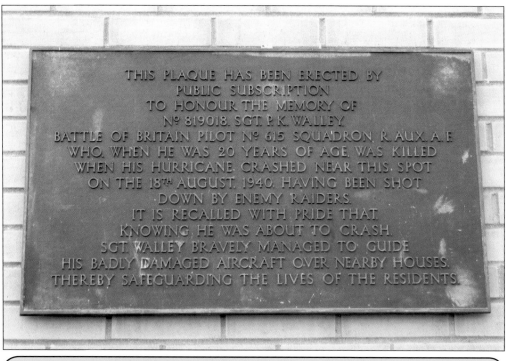

THIS PLAQUE HAS BEEN ERECTED BY
PUBLIC SUBSCRIPTION
TO HONOUR THE MEMORY OF
Nº 819018. SGT. P. K. WALLEY.
BATTLE OF BRITAIN PILOT Nº 615 SQUADRON, R. AUX. A. F.
WHO, WHEN HE WAS 20 YEARS OF AGE, WAS KILLED
WHEN HIS HURRICANE CRASHED NEAR THIS SPOT
ON THE 18ᵀᴴ AUGUST 1940. HAVING BEEN SHOT
DOWN BY ENEMY RAIDERS.
IT IS RECALLED WITH PRIDE THAT,
KNOWING HE WAS ABOUT TO CRASH,
SGT. WALLEY BRAVELY MANAGED TO GUIDE
HIS BADLY DAMAGED AIRCRAFT OVER NEARBY HOUSES,
THEREBY SAFEGUARDING THE LIVES OF THE RESIDENTS.

18 August 1940

Hurricane, P2768 KW - J	**Time: 13.30**
615 Squadron	Pilot:
Location:	Sergeant Peter Kenneth Walley (20)
Morden Park, Morden	killed

Peter Walley

Peter Walley had joined the RAF in 1938 as an Aircrafthand and air gunner, joining 615 Squadron in August that year. Like many others in his position he was given the opportunity to re-train as a pilot shortly before war was declared and on 6 August 1940 he reported back to 615 Squadron as a fully fledged fighter pilot.

On 16 August he made his first and only combat claim; for a 'share' in the probable destruction of an Me109. Two days later, on 18 August, he was not down to fly, but he had talked his way onto the duty roster and was scrambled as number 2 in the Section led by Squadron Leader Kayll. Peter was seen dashing out of a hut with his flying helmet and his radio transmitter leads in his hands, yelling, 'Start me up somebody'.

A plaque was mounted on the wall of Merton College to commemorate the heroic action of Peter Walley.

Sergeant Peter Walley, No.615 Squadron.

A few minutes later, with a burst of throttle and in a cloud of dust he taxied his Hurricane KW-J out of the pen and across the field to catch the others.

Once airborne they were ordered to patrol Hawkinge, then head north east and keep a lookout for fighters. At 26,000 feet the squadron was attacked by Me109s over Sutton. Three Hurricanes went down in this attack; Hugo, the Section Leader, Pilot Officer Looker and Peter Walley. Looker reported that he had seen Walley's Hurricane turn right over and go down in flames. A fourth member of the squadron, Elmer Gaunce, was shot down in a separate engagement near Sevenoaks.

The circumstances of this loss, however, are not straightforward and eyewitness accounts reveal conflicting detail. It is possible that the fire seen by Looker went out and that he regained control. It may have been that he was trapped in his aircraft and unable to bale out, or he may have believed that his safest option was to force-land, as Simpson had elected to do that day.

Either way, several people in Merton saw the crippled Hurricane as it came out of the haze. It cleared high-tension cables and then flew at rooftop height right across the St Helier Estate, and disappeared behind rooftops. The aircraft was then seen to turn sharply to starboard to avoid houses along the London Road, it lost speed, stalled, and the nose dropped.

The final crash may have been due to the pilot being injured, or nursing a barely controllable machine, or perhaps the fuel ran out and the engine failed a moment too soon. Whatever the cause, the Hurricane fell away behind trees to crash on the edge of Morden Park. Peter Walley was killed instantly. Within days letters from notable locals were received by the Air Ministry, all praising the heroism of the pilot who had steered his aircraft away from the houses, and who lost his life in doing so. In 1972 Group Captain Leonard Cheshire VC, of Cheshire Homes fame, unveiled a plaque on the newly built Merton Technical College in honour of Peter Walley. The plaque is said to be sited within yards of where the aircraft fell.

18 August 1940

Dornier Do17Z
Wn. 2504, F1+IH, 1./KG76

Location:
Mill Lane, Hurst Green

Time: 13.30

Crew:
Oberleutnant Walther Stoldt (pilot) - killed
Feldwebel P. Gengel - killed
Oberleutnant W. Surk (Kriegsberichter) killed
Oberfeldwebel W. Lautersack baled out and captured, injured
Feldwebel J. Beck baled out and captured, injured

Mr and Mrs Addison lived with their own two children and two evacuee children in Warren Cottage, a detached property built in 1845 on Warren Lane, Hurst Green. Hearing the approaching aircraft, they searched the sky to see the formation of bombers coming from the direction of Edenbridge; and a single fighter aircraft seemingly climbing to meet them head-on. The fighter pilot fired at the lead bomber and it fell out of the formation, trailing smoke. As the Addisons looked on, two parachutes opened and a third man jumped, but his parachute failed as the bomber circled Oxted to the south of them. Then the bomber turned towards them and started to fall at a steep angle until the pilot appeared to regain control only a few hundred feet above the ground. Transfixed by the spectacle of the rapidly approaching bomber Mr Addison saw it strike the ground near the sewage farm, just yards from his cottage. He recalled in 1960:

"It hit the ground so fast that it started to disintegrate in a sheet of flame, striking some trees it careered through a hedge and bounced partly over the cottage into a field. All that was in its path including the cottage was sprayed with blazing fuel. Mrs Addison was in the house with the four children, their only escape from the flames was via the window of a downstairs bathroom. The dog, however, rushed out from the kitchen door into the blaze and disappeared. Miraculously the petrol fire was soon burnt out and only the hedge and woodwork of the cottage were left alight. The house had suffered only superficial damage."

Three views of Warren Cottage taken by Dennis Knight in 1960 showing where the Dornier crashed. The cottage has since been demolished to make way for a housing estate.

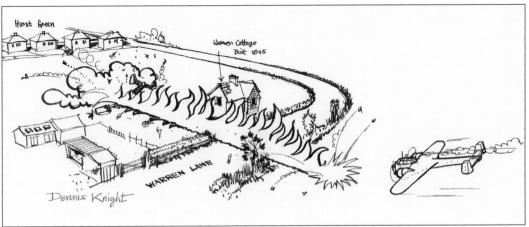

Dennis Knight's sketch illustrating the path taken by the Dornier in its last moments.

The Dornier had been carrying a full load of bombs and these had been scattered over the fields behind Warren Cottage. One however, had smashed through the wall of the cottage and lodged under the kitchen sink. Canadian soldiers were quickly on the scene and for some half an hour confusion reigned. The Canadians actually started discharging a light machine-gun into the wreckage. One engine from the bomber had bounced and rolled along the ground for some 200 yards, finally coming to rest in the gardens of some cottages at Hurst Green. Two smouldering bodies, that of the pilot Oberleutnant Stoldt and another man lay amongst the wreckage. Mr Addison found a steel helmet in the wreck and a flying boot marked with the name Eric Wiesman. The body of another crewman fell at Guildables Lane with his unopened parachute.

A happy sequel to this story was the finding of the dog, some mile or so from the scene. It was in a pitiful state with fur burnt off, burnt pads, nose and ears. A local vet took the poor animal away. Six weeks later the dog was returned to Mr and Mrs Addison, healed and sporting little white booties to protect the newly healed pads. His nose that was previously black was now pink! The vet refused to accept any payment for his kindness to the animal.

Dornier Do17Z-2
Wn. 0334, F1+HT, 9./KG76

Location:
Golf Road, Kenley

Time: 13.30

Crew:
Oberleutnant Hans Siegfried Ahrends (25) - killed
Oberst Dr. Otto Sommer (48) - killed
Unteroffizier Johannes Dietz (24) - killed
Feldwebel Karl Greulich (29) - killed
Feldwebel Johannes Petersen (26) killed

The houses of Highleigh and Sunny Croft on Golf Road were inside the wartime boundary of Kenley Airfield and the owners had to show their identity cards when they passed through the barrier across the road to go into town. There had been lots of air raid warnings and Mrs Marshall of Highleigh was little perturbed when the sirens sounded once more. She had been standing in her garden when the Hurricanes took off only feet above her head and an airman had shouted at her to take cover when the warning came, but it was only when she heard the bombers approaching that she scrambled into a little shelter at the foot of some trees. The noise quickly became appalling; aircraft engines, guns and exploding bombs caused the ground under her feet to rock.

When the raid was over she emerged from the shelter to find a shell or bomb had fallen harmlessly only feet from her, fires were burning on the airfield and men ran shouting everywhere. At the top of Golf Road a bomber had crashed into the bungalow named Sunny Croft, belonging to Mr and Mrs Turner-Smith. The bungalow was on fire and parts of the Dornier were strewn in its gardens, but its owners scrambled out of the rubble with only slight injuries. Later that day Mr Turner-Smith was able to pose in the shambles of his bungalow and told a reporter from Evening News. "I don't know why I'm still alive!" He had Sunny Croft rebuilt in 1947 and lived there for another four years.

Two views of Sunny Croft; August 1940 and shortly after it was rebuilt.

THE AIR BATTLES OVER BRITAIN—*VIVID* PICTURES

30th August, 1940

THE WAR

No. 45

3D WEEKLY

Incorporating WAR PICTORIAL

HOME GUARD SHOOT DOWN NAZI RAIDER

The Berlin Press has sneered at the Home Guard as "hedge-snipers." But last week members of the Home Guard proved that they could "snipe" to some effect when they brought down a Dornier bomber by rifle fire. The Nazi plane was machine-gunning a common in a South London suburb. Twenty Home Guards in an emplacement near by "let him have it" with 180 rounds. The Dornier was hit and crashed. This impression by a WAR WEEKLY artist shows our "spare-time soldiers" at it.

27TH AUGUST 1940

27 August 1940

Heinkel He111 H-2
Wn. 5376, V4+CD, Stab III./KG1
Location:
21 Manor Avenue, Caterham

Time: 02.45 hours

Crew:
**Major W. Fanelsa
(Gruppenkommandeur) - PoW
Feldwebel Friedrich Meyer - PoW
Oberfeldwebel Eric Braunsburger - PoW
Oberfeldwebel Arthur Vetter - PoW
Gefreiter G. Zimpel - PoW**

The air raid warning sirens sounded again in the Caterham area in the early hours. Mr Hayes followed his usual routine when the wailing of the warning was heard and led his family to their refuge in a cupboard under the stairs of their home in Manor Avenue. Their house backed on to Queens Park recreation ground with its large expanse of grass and substantial trees. The August night was warm and humid in the confines of the small cupboard, an uncomfortable experience for Mr Hayes, his wife, son and the pet dog.

At around half-past two the family clearly heard the gunfire of the local anti-aircraft battery open fire for a few minutes and the drone of aircraft engines passing overhead; then the silence of the early morning returned. The all clear would soon sound and then the family could return to their beds.

Suddenly the Hayes family's world disintegrated around them. With the sound of splintering wood, breaking glass and tumbling masonry their house shook. Though safe under the supporting structure of the stairs Mr Hayes pushed open the cupboard door to see what had happened. Through the darkness he made his way to a bedroom at the rear of the house overlooking the park. The roaring and crackling sound of a fire was now clearly audible. The heavy blackout curtains kept the room dark and Mr Hayes had to peer through a gap to see the terrific blaze outside.

The scene at Manor Avenue on the morning after the Heinkel crashed.

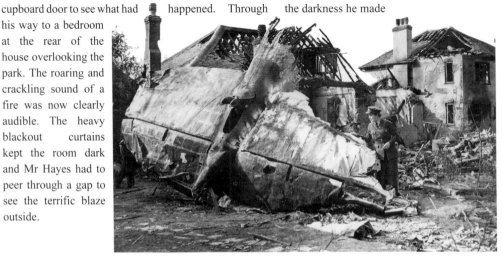

He ran to the telephone and called the fire brigade before returning to his family in the cupboard, where he waited until a fireman called them to come out of their house. Hastily grabbing a few belongings the family left their home to the accompaniment of bullets exploding in the fire. Fortunately the house was saved.

Outside, the full extent of the damage was clear. Parts of a German bomber lay scattered and burning. The bungalow next door was burning and its roof had been torn off. Mr Iwankriens, a tall bearded Dutchman and his sister-in-law were standing in their night clothes as firemen battled to put out the flames engulfing their home. They had escaped with their lives, but had lost everything save for a little jewellery.

Major Fanelsa, captain of the Heinkel.

Mr Philips, an assistant master at a local school and Home Guard member, was disturbed from his reading by the ringing of a telephone bell; there were enemy parachutists at large. Taking his revolver from a drawer, he set out to patrol the grounds of his school and almost immediately found one of the German airmen, who he led away at gunpoint.

Mr Elphinstone, Company Commander of the Home Guard, was leading a handful of his men to the point where two more parachutes had been descending in a searchlight beam. He found the men walking along a residential road in the middle of Caterham valley, and formally arrested both. The remaining two airmen landed neatly in a nest of soldiers and saved them the trouble of searching for them.

Another view of the burnt out tail section of V4+CD

Major Fanelsa, commanding officer of III./KG1, had led the five Heinkels from their airfield at Montdidier in France the previous evening. Their target had been the factories of Coventry. On their return, Fanelsa's bomber had been hit by the anti-aircraft fire from 148th Anti Aircraft Battery led by Sergeant Longman at Caterham and it was so damaged that he gave his crew the order to bale out.

The abandoned aircraft, apparently with two dead engines, came down on an even keel and struck the ground in Queens Park at a terrific speed. It skidded across the grass heading directly for the house of Mr Hayes and would have crashed straight into it had it not hit a large tree that slewed the bomber round and caused it to disintegrate, sending a sheet of blazing fuel over the houses.

30TH AUGUST 1940

The Battle of Britain entered a yet more aggressive phase on this day as the Luftwaffe launched more heavy attacks on RAF airfields. The skies were clear, thanks to an anti-cyclone over Europe, and vast armadas of bombers escorted by swarms of protecting Me109s were heavily engaged over Kent by late morning. Some aircraft penetrated further inland bringing large-scale battles to Surrey's skies once again.

The first action of the day over Surrey involved South African Edward 'Teddy' Morris, up with Biggin Hill's No. 79 Squadron ordered to intercept the Heinkels of KG1 bound for Farnborough. 'Teddy' had built a reputation during the 18 months he had been with the squadron of having nerves of steel; they almost got the better of him over Newdigate.

Morris chose to make a head-on pass at a Heinkel that had been separated from the formation by a previous attack. Closing at frightening speed he had just a second to open fire with his eight Brownings before he or his enemy must break away to avoid a head-on collision at 500 miles an hour. 'Teddy' fired. His target bore straight towards him as the bullets hit the cockpit. Then the two collided.

This part of the Heinkel's wing would have made a handsome trophy!

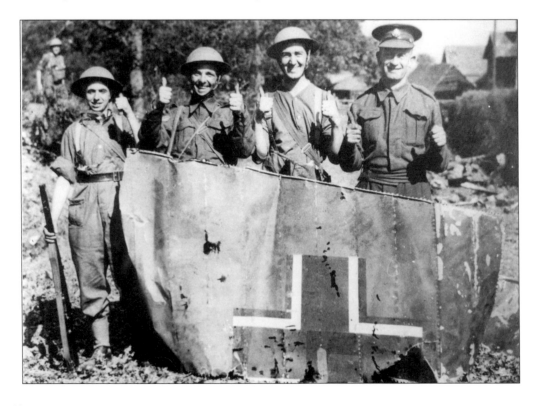

The Swires Farm dairy herd examine a new feature of their pasture - Morris' Hurricane.

Miraculously the Hurricane glanced off the bomber, but both aircraft were seriously damaged and out of control.

Owner of Swires Farm, Mr Spiller, saw two parachutes from the Heinkel open and one of its wings break off, sending it into a corkscrew spin to earth with three more men inside. It landed near the farm buildings and began to burn, causing bullets to explode.

One of the farm workers suggested to Mrs Spiller and her daughter that they should leave the house and take refuge in the properly constructed shelter behind the house. No sooner had she got in than the first of four bombs exploded, doing considerable damage.

Captain McIntosh, a doctor with the 1st Canadian Division, with a fellow captain ran to the where the wing had fallen at the bottom of Henfold Hill, determined to secure a souvenir. They set to work on a white painted cross, but were thwarted by the rivets that held it firmly in place and left hurriedly with only a small piece when a local policeman arrived on his bicycle.

Rudolf Bass had been badly injured in the attack and landed at North Holmwood. He was taken to Dorking General Hospital suffering from head and eye injuries and was transferred to the Royal Naval Hospital Woolwich the following day.

30 August 1940

Heinkel He111 H-2
Wn. 2720, V4+BV
10./KG1

Location:
Swires Farm, Capel

Time: 11.22 hours

Crew:
**Oberleutnant Paul Fröhlisch (pilot) - PoW
Hauptmann Rudolf Bäss (observer)
PoW, very badly wounded
Oberfeldwebel Waldemar Hornig
(wireless operator) (26) - killed
Gefreiter Dr Karl Heimel (gunner) (23)
killed
Oberfeldwebel Gunter Stahlberg
(mechanic) (28) - killed**

30 August 1940

Hurricane, P3203
79 Squadron (Biggin Hill)
Location:
**Brookfield Copse, near
Swires Farm, Capel**

Time: 11.22 hours

Pilot:
**Flying Officer Edward James Morris (25)
baled out, injured**

'TEDDY' MORRIS

South African 'Teddy' Morris joined the RAF in 1937 and had been with 79 Squadron since January 1939. Following the collision Morris escaped by parachute and landed near Dorking, then returned to Biggin Hill. The following day, although not scheduled to fly, he scrambled to intercept Dorniers over Kent and crash-landed his damaged Hurricane; this time he was hospitalised by his injuries. He later went to the Middle East as a fighter pilot and held senior staff posts until he retired from the RAF in 1968 as an Air Commodore.

Wreckage of the Heinkel was blasted over a huge area by the explosion.

253 SQUADRON – A BAPTISM OF FIRE

As the ground crews of No.253 Squadron finished unpacking from the previous day's move from Prestwick in Scotland, the first six of the squadron's Hurricanes lifted from Kenley's runway. Five minutes later another seven pilots of 253 took off to intercept the enemy. Within hours of its arrival the squadron was in action, and over the following few days the pilots of 253 would be entwined with the story of Surrey's Battle.

At 11.30 the pilots of No. 253 Squadron flew into battle for the first time. Immediately 'B' Flight engaged the bombers over north Kent and Pilot Officer Nowak claimed an aircraft he believed to have been a Ju86 as destroyed. 'A' Flight was right behind and Pilot Officer Greenwood latched on to a Heinkel that he riddled with bullets until it was obliged to land at Haxted Mead Farm on the Kent /Surrey border.

PILOTS WITH 253 SQUADRON

S/Ldr Starr	Shot down and killed 31/8/40, Eastry, Kent.
P/O Corkett	Survived.
P/O Murch	Crashed 9/9/40. Shot down and baled out 9/10/40 injured. Died of illness in India in 1943
P/O Greenwood	Survived.
P/O Strang	Survived.
P/O Clifton	Shot down and killed, 1/9/40, Staplehurst, Kent.
F/Lt Cambridge	Baled out at Kingsnorth, Kent, 6/9/40, but died.
Sgt Innes	Shot down and crashed 20 September. Crashed again 11/10/40. Survived.
P/O Samolinski	Shot down and killed over the Channel, 26/9/40.
F/Lt Wedgewood	Killed December 1942.
P/O Jenkins	Shot down and killed 30/8/40 at Woldingham, Surrey.
P/O Nowak	Crashed 17/10/40. Shot down and killed September 1941.
P/O Francis	Shot down and killed 30/8/40 at Wrotham, Kent.
P/O Carthew	Survived.
F/O Watts	Survived.
Sgt Dredge	Shot down and burned in April 1941 near Malta. Killed in a flying accident in May 1945.
P/O Bell-Salter	Shot down 2/9/40 and badly injured. Survived.
S/Ldr Gleave	Shot down 31/8/40 and badly burned. Survived.
F/Lt Brown	Shot down and injured 30/8/40 near Maidstone. Survived.
Sgt Cooper	Shot down and baled out 30/8/40 at Biddenden, Kent. Survived.
Sgt Dickinson	Shot down and killed 30/8/40, over Dungeness.
Sgt Kee	Shot down and crashed 15/10/40. Killed over Yugoslavia April1944.

Of the 22 pilots who flew on 30 August 1940, 7 were killed in the Battle,
5 were killed later in the war and 10 survived the war – 2 with serious injuries.
15 pilots were shot down at least once during the Battle of Britain.

The pilots then became embroiled in a running fight that ranged over a wide area; Flight Lieutenant Cambridge followed a Bf110 he had attacked down to 2,000 feet and left it going straight down with no chance of recovery, Pilot Officer Samolinski attacked two Bf110s and sent one down in a spiral dive, Sergeant Innes saw 'his' Bf110 roll on to its back and dive into the ground.

---

30 August 1940

Heinkel He111 H-2,
Wn. 3305, V4+HV, 5./KG1

Location:
Haxted Mead Farm, Nr Lingfield

Time: 11.35 hours

Crew:
Feldwebel Heinz Schnabel (pilot) - PoW
Gefreiter Hans Groth (observer) - PoW
Unteroffizier Ernst Paeslack
(wireless operator) - wounded, PoW
Unteroffizier Erich Stärk (mechanic)-PoW
Gefreiter W Reis (gunner) - killed

INTERROGATION REPORT

About 20 aircraft started at 10.15 hours from Arvillers
(mid-way between Rosiers and Montdidier).

Objective stated to be hangars on Farnborough Aerodrome. 24 x 50kg bombs.

Course: Arvillers-landfall south of Dover-Ashford, Tonbridge Railway-Farnborough.
Height 13,000 feet.

Objective attained and bombed, but results not observed, as were attacked immediately
by Spitfires. Both engines shot up, slight fire started but went out, and made
a forced landing in reasonably good condition.

This was the aircraft attacked by John 'Percy' Greenwood. He followed the Heinkel down, saw it make a belly landing and flew so low that could see the crew climb out, one of them covered in blood. This man was probably W Reis who died shortly after in Redhill Country Hospital. The other injured man, Ernst Paeslack, was taken by car to Edenbridge Hospital and the remaining three were held at a searchlight post at Chellows until they were taken away for interrogation.

John had been born in 1921 and grew up in the Richmond and Kingston area of Surrey. He joined the RAF early in 1939, quickly learned to fly and joined 253 Squadron in time for the Battle of France.

After the Battle of Britain he flew fighters in India and had a thoroughly miserable time. In 1950 he sailed for Australia and eventually became an airline pilot among other jobs before he settled near Perth.

Heinz Schnabel pulled off a good landing at Haxted in his bullet riddled bomber.

Also airborne and leading the 'Emergency Section' was Squadron Leader Gleave with his numbers 2 and 3, Flight Lieutenant Brown and Pilot Officer Colin Francis. Gleave later wrote,

"Suddenly tracers whistled over my head. A glance in my mirror told me that there was a 109 on my tail and about 200 yards astern. I jinked, dipping to starboard and then pulling up again in a sharp climbing turn to port. There were no signs of my No. 1 or No. 2, but by then it was impossible to tell friend from foe at a distance, for the Hun fighters were flying at a variety of levels and there was a lot of firing going on – at what, it was difficult to see."

Gleave and his fellow pilots claimed to have brought down four Messerschmitts in the combat, but both Brown and Francis were shot down.

PILOT OFFICER COLIN FRANCIS – LOST FOR 40 YEARS

Colin Francis came from Stoke D'Abernon in Surrey. He joined the squadron as it re-built after the Battle of France and became a firm friend of Pilot Officer Carthew, the pair becoming known as 'Tweedledum and Tweedledee'. Colin was one of the squadron's pilots not to return from their first sortie; in fact nothing was heard of him for forty years.

The wreck of his Hurricane, L1965, was not identified at the time and his body remained buried with it under a field at Wrotham Hill, Kent.

In 1980 the Hurricane's wreck was discovered and identified, leading to Colin's funeral on 29 September, 1981, at Brookwood Military Cemetery, Surrey.

His friend, the Canadian Carthew, was reportedly so distressed about the loss of Colin that he never flew again.

Colin Francis came from Stoke D'Abernon. Although his body was not discovered in 1940, he was commemorated at his local church, St Mary The Virgin.

Pilot Officer David Jenkins.

High over Woldingham a winding dogfight developed between 253's Hurricanes and Messerschmitts. A 109's gunfire set the Hurricane of 21-year-old Scotsman David Jenkins alight and he was forced to take to his parachute. What happened next has been the cause of debate amongst historians ever since, for his bullet ridden body landed by parachute in Marden Park. It has variously been suggested that he was unfortunate enough to be hit just he was getting out of the cockpit, or was deliberately machine gunned as he hung helpless in his parachute.

Also falling from the sky in the same area were two Messerschmitt pilots from the same unit, Oberleutnant Hans Rath and Leutnant Rudolf Ziegler; they had collided in the air when both attempted to get on the tail of the same Hurricane.

Jenkins had joined 253 Squadron in November 1939. He had baled out of a Hurricane when he lost control in cloud at night over Scotland in August and landed safely by parachute. He was shot down in his first combat.

30 August 1940

Hurricane, P3921,
253 Squadron (Kenley)
Location:
**Butlers Dene Road,
Woldingham**

Time: 11.45 hours
Pilot:
**Pilot Officer David Nicholas Owen
Jenkins (21) - baled out but died of
bullet wounds.**

David Jenkins's
Hurricane fell into a
garden at Woldingham.
Small parts were
discovered in an
excavation in the
1980s.

30 August 1940

Messerschmitt Bf109E-4,
Wn. 6072, White 6+, 4./JG54
Location:
Fickleshole Farm, Chelsham

Time: 11.45 hours
Pilot:
Oberleutnant Hans Rath - baled out and captured at Granville Road, Limpsfield

INTERROGATION REPORT

Started at 11.20 hours on a freelance patrol.
Was getting into position to attack a Hurricane, when he was rammed by some other aircraft, which cut off the tail. He baled out from nearly 20,000 feet.

30 August 1940

Messerschmitt Bf109E-4
Wn. 1643, Stab II/JG54
Location:
Layhams Farm, Addington

Time: 11.45 hours
Pilot:
Leutnant Rudolf Ziegler - baled out and landed on the roof of 'Meadowside' Detillens Lane, Limpsfield

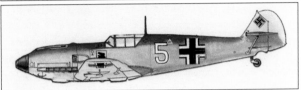

Oberleutnant Hans Rath 'White 6' and Leutnant Rudolf Ziegler 'White 5' collided in the combat over east Surrey. (Dennis Knight)

A press photographer visited Layhams Farm the next day and found soldiers and airmen picking over the wreckage.

30 August 1940

Spitfire, L1012
616 Squadron (Kenley)

Time: 12.10 hours

Location:
Near Caterham bypass roundabout

Pilot:
**Sergeant J Hopewell - safe,
Overshot Kenley and force landed.**

For the second day running the Luftwaffe launched mass attacks with Me109 escorts, this constant pressure giving the RAF, and 253 at Kenley, no time to recover from the previous day's activity.

Erprobungsgruppe 210 returned to Croydon again at lunchtime, just as the twelve pilots of No.85 Squadron took off to intercept them. Led by Peter Townsend, the Hurricanes left as the bombs fell around them and they struggled to climb and catch the raiders; which they did over Tunbridge Wells. Townsend's Hurricane was hit by cannon fire in the combat and he baled out, having been hit in his left foot. Later he had his left big toe amputated. This time the damage to the airfield was not as bad as their previous effort on 15 August, but one hangar and a lorry were destroyed.

A number of He111s made to attack Biggin Hill and caused yet more damage to the badly hit airfield, but seven pilots of 253 Squadron caught them and shot down one bomber as they fled towards the coast. Scattered by the combat the squadron's pilots returned to Kenley separately and Squadron Tom Gleave was attacked from behind by an Me109. Gleave's Hurricane burst into flames and he was horrifically burnt before he managed to parachute. He became celebrated as one to most famous of Archie Mckindoe's plastic surgery 'Guinea Pigs'. Thus 253 Squadron lost its second Commanding Officer in two days. Another 253 pilot, Alec Trueman, crash-landed his damaged Hurricane at Sanderstead and escaped unscathed.

---

31 August 1940

Hurricane, P3714
253 Squadron
Location:
Limpsfield Road, Sanderstead

Time: 09.30 hours
Pilot:
Pilot Officer Alec Albert Gray Trueman (26) - safe

---

31 August 1940

Hurricane, N2345
79 Squadron
Location:
Water Lane, Limpsfield

Time: 09.30 hours
Pilot:
Pilot Officer George Hassall Nelson-Edwards (22) - injured

Nelson-Edwards had read history at Oxford where he learned to fly with the University Air Squadron. Already an experienced fighter pilot by this time, he damaged an Me109 but his Hurricane was hit and he crash landed. He had leg injuries but was safe, and the aircraft was wrecked beyond repair.

Returning to his squadron he shot down an He111 off the Irish coast on 29 September, but was shot down again, this time taking to his parachute. He later became an instructor and returned to combat in 1942 over North Africa leading 93 Squadron. He left the RAF in 1960 as a Wing Commander.

31 August 1940

Hurricane, V7200
79 Squadron
Location:
Halliloo Farm, Woldingham

Time: 13.10 hours
Pilot:
**Flight Sergeant Henry Albert Bolton (21)
killed**

Henry Bolton from Hartlepool completed his training in July and was posted to 79 Squadron in August. He was lost on one of his first combat flights.

Mr and Mrs Deacon set off to visit Kingswood and Banstead on what proved to be an eventful Sunday morning. Several air raid alerts sounded and German aircraft were about, one of which machine-gunned civilians at Kingswood. By the time the couple reached Banstead at lunch-time aircraft were fighting overhead and an aircraft went down in flames, a parachute then opened and the pilot floated down, but this was not the last event to leave an impression on them. As they were making their way home to Woldingham they came upon the wreck of a Hurricane at Mr Fuller's farm. The aircraft was riddled with bullet holes; even the propeller blades were dented and perforated by them.

Mr Fuller recalled the event to Dennis Knight in 1961. The family had seen the pilot seeking a place to land his damaged aircraft as he flew very low down the valley from the south-east. The pilot had flown into a trap, for ahead of him the valley turned and became more densely populated, leaving him little option but to turn around and head back up the valley.

Soldiers guarding the wreck of Bolton's Hurricane practiced their skipping skills with a belt of .303 ammunition!

The aircraft turned 180 degrees to port and made as if to land on the sloping meadows between High Lane and Bughills Farm, but right in its path was Halliloo Farm, nestling in the valley bottom with a screen of tall pine trees and the farmhouse perched on the northern slope.

The aircraft climbed a little to clear the trees; then crashed to the ground. The Hurricane had fallen not more than 100 yards from the farmhouse and

55

Mr Fuller rushed with his brother to help its pilot. Mr Deacon also rushed to help. The pilot was alive, but unconscious and had only a weak pulse, his legs were trapped in the mangled wreck and he had a bullet wound in his back. The men tried desperately to free the pilot, cutting away the harness and pulling at the wreckage, but he died still trapped in his cockpit.

---

31 August 1940

Messerschmitt Bf109E-7
Wn. 5600, 3./LG2
Location:
Chathill Park Farm
Tandridge

Time: 18.45 hours
Pilot:
Oberleutnant Hasso von Perthes - baled
out and captured at Hurst Green, but
died of his injuries.

Early in the evening another combat took place, this time over Tandridge. The victim this time was Oberleutnant Hasso von Perthes, an Me109 pilot, who had the misfortune to encounter the aggressive Polish pilots of No.303 Squadron on one of their first sorties.

The Messerschmitt had been set on fire by Pilot Officer Feric and von Perthes took to his parachute but, according to legend, the Poles went into a line-astern formation and took turns at shooting at him as he swung in his parachute. As with Pilot Officer Jenkins the previous day, he may well have been struck as he exited his aircraft, but Mr Payne, who saw the incident, recalled vividly that he saw the RAF fighters attacking the German pilot.

Mr Payne who incorporated a machine-gun into his garden wall!

Whatever the circumstances, Hasso von Perthes' parachute became entangled with telephone wires at Hurst Green and he had several bullet wounds. He was rushed to a local hospital for surgery and later transferred to the Royal Herbert Hospital, Woolwich, where he succumbed to his injuries on 14 September.

Mr Payne's son went to where the Messerschmitt had crashed at Chathill Park Farm and brought home some 'souvenirs' which his father made him leave in the garden as they were 'smelling'. Eventually most of the parts were lost, but the resourceful builder used a machine-gun as part of a wall he was building. 25 years later he knocked the wall down and retrieved the gun in the presence of the celebrated American Sunday Times photographer Robert Freson.

LG2 pilots line up with their mascot dog and an Me109 in the background.

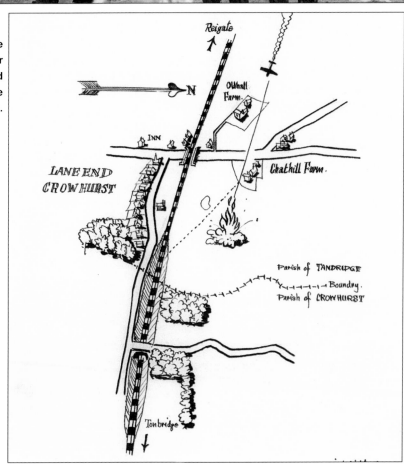

Dennis Knight's sketch showing where von Perthes' Me109 fell.

1ST SEPTEMBER 1940

The fighter pilots at Croydon and Kenley, like those at the other airfields in south-east England, had come under terrific strain in the past two weeks. What would this Sunday bring? The day had started with some light cloud diffusing the sun, but by midday the clouds had largely dispersed and once again the sun beat down upon the pilots as they awaited the next call to scramble. It had been another taxing day; two scrambles already for most of them, to intercept Heinkels and Dorniers over Kent and the Thames.

Shortly after lunch the pilots of Croydon's No.85 Squadron scrambled to intercept another force, estimated to be between 150 and 200 aircraft, as it approached Biggin Hill. As the Hurricanes climbed over Kenley they were 'bounced' by a group of Me109s. The formation was being led by the 24 year-old Battle of France veteran Patrick Woods-Scawen, but even with his great experience they were caught completely unaware. The German fighter pilots came from above and passed through the squadron of Hurricanes that was 'cut to pieces'. Within minutes six Hurricanes were falling from the sky over Kenley and towards Tunbridge.

A section of No.79 Squadron was up from Biggin Hill when it was also 'bounced' by Me109s as two of the pilots recalled:

"There had been a lot of activity already on Sunday 1ˢᵗ September and the readiness aircraft were airborne. At about mid-day an order came through to scramble all available aircraft to patrol over Biggin at 20,000 feet. There were only two aircraft, mine W6670 and the other flown by Brian Noble.

We took off and gained height and at about 17,000 feet saw a mass of aircraft with fighter cover above us and heading for London. We climbed to their height and identified about 30 Dornier 17s with Me109s behind and above. Brian Noble was echelon starboard to me.

I got a Dornier in my sights and pressed the firing button when tracer fire started overtaking me from behind. I felt a thump on the leg and a fire started down by the right rudder pedal. Flames started building up in the cockpit so I decided to quit. The next thing I remember is being on the end of a parachute – some Me109s milling around and another parachute not far away.

A Hurricane was in a vertical dive in flames – probably mine. I landed at Dunton Green. I am not sure where my aircraft ended up. The other parachute had Brian Noble on the end – he landed in the Marley lake at Riverhead."

TREVOR BRYANT-FENN

"I remember being recalled from the Officer's Mess after a vain attempt to eat a hurried luncheon and being 'scrambled' immediately on arriving back at dispersal. Subsequently, during the climb we intercepted a large Luftwaffe bomber formation

and made a somewhat hurried attack, although to what effect I do not remember as I found myself crossing through the bomber formation (height 12-15,000 feet) and surrounded by enemy aircraft and tracer and cannon fire, whilst turning left to run through the formation I felt a dull thud and simultaneously saw a burst of flame below my feet indicating a hit in the main fuel tank in front of the instrument panel.

My remaining memory is of releasing the locking pin on my harness, pushing the stick hard forward to convert the left turn into a 'bunt', the effect of which was to project me out of the cockpit; fortunately the preamble to an attack was to slide the canopy back to allow for just such a hurried exit!

I recall having some trouble pulling the parachute ripcord – my hands having been burned – and I lost some nails on both hands. I recall only two brief moments whilst parachuting down – one of being close to another parachuting airman at one time, whilst both of us were 'investigated' by a friendly fighter and secondly of being over water into which I fell almost immediately.

This in fact was the Marley sand and gravel pit at Riverhead, Sevenoaks and from which I was promptly rescued by the local LDV, one of whom took me to the local hospital at Sevenoaks, where I was to spend the next month in company with Trevor Bryant-Fenn, my section leader on that sortie."

BRIAN NOBLE

A Hurricane of 85 Squadron.

It would seem that Trevor Bryant-Fenn's Hurricane fell near Biggin Hill, but Brian Noble's aircraft flew on a few miles west and eventually crashed near Hooley. Of the Hurricanes lost, four fell in Surrey:

1 September 1940

Hurricane, P3150
85 Squadron
Location:
Zig-Zag Road, Kenley

Time: 14.08 hours
Pilot:
Flying Officer Patrick Philip Woods-Scawen DFC (24) - killed

Leading the squadron, Patrick Woods-Scawen's Hurricane was seen to spiral down and crash in a meadow between Welcomes Road and Hermitage Road, not far from Kenley airfield.

Police and ARP reported the crash and the local fire brigade put out the burning grass, but there was no sign of the pilot's body. It was hoped that he had managed to bale out and that he would appear again in the mess that evening, but he did not.

As the days passed hope for Patrick faded until the evening of the 5th, when news reached the squadron that the pilot's body had been found at a house called 'The Ivies' in Kenley Lane. He had been found in thick undergrowth with his parachute unopened.

Patrick Woods-Scawen, sometimes known as 'Woody', was one of two brothers to serve in the Battle of Britain. He had been born in Karachi, India, but the family were living in Farnborough, Hampshire, in 1940. His younger brother Charles Anthony 'Tony' was also a Hurricane pilot, serving with No.43 Squadron. By a curious and tragic quirk of fate Tony was shot down by a 109 the very day after Patrick. Tony also baled out, but again his parachute failed to open and he was killed. Thus their mother, Kathleen, and father, Philip, had to bear the news that both their sons had been killed within hours of each other.

An 85 Squadron Hurricane at readiness.

There was third member of the extended Woods-Scawen family who was also lost while serving with the RAF. He was Gerald Woods-Scawen, a pilot with No.92 Squadron who died 3 October 1941 in Norway. He was the 19 year-old son of John and Rose Woods-Scawen, also of Farnborough.

1 September 1940

Hurricane, L2071 VY-O	**Time: 14.08 hours**
85 Squadron	Pilot:
Location:	**Sergeant Glendon Bulmar Booth (19)**
Kingswood, Sanderstead	**died of his injuries five months later**

Glendon Booth did not fit the traditional view of the upper-class university airman. He was from the London suburb of Sydenham and went to Brockley County School; then went to work for the London Electricity Company before enrolling in the RAF Volunteer Reserve.

As he faithfully kept formation with Patrick Woods-Scawen and the others of his squadron the 20mm cannon shells from the Messerschmitts struck home with devastating effect. Fire broke out in his cockpit; Glendon had only seconds to get out. He slid back the Hurricane's hood, unfastened his Sutton harness and pushed himself out of the cockpit, away from the intense heat.

Below, the residents of Sanderstead had been alerted by the noise of aircraft engines and the crackling of gunfire that disturbed their sunny Sunday afternoon's rest. Mothers and fathers shouted at their children to take cover and get into the shelters once more. Some, hypnotised by the enormous spectacle of the occasion, squinted into the brilliant light to catch a glimpse of the combat that suddenly erupted above their heads.

Nineteen year old Sergeant Glendon Booth.

A half-opened parachute caught the eye of some; below hung a pilot coming down towards them very fast. The pilot had one shoe on and one off, his clothing was tattered and flapping behind him as he collided with a telephone pole and then fell onto a rose arch at 115 Littleheath Road. Men women and children gathered round the badly injured pilot. A cannon shell had hit his parachute pack, damaging it so that the canopy failed to deploy correctly, his high-speed landing had broken a leg, and arm, and fractured his spine.

In time the clattering bell of an ambulance announced its arrival and Glendon was taken away to Purley Hospital. His back injury had paralysed him, but he fought for life until succumbing to a kidney infection five months later. His parents buried their son at Crystal Palace Cemetery, Beckenham where they, in their turn, chose to be buried at his side.

1 September 1940

Hurricane, V7343
85 Squadron
Location:
Merstham

Time: 14.08 hours
Pilot:
Flying Officer Arthur Vincent Gowers
(27) - injured

Another victim of the surprise Messerschmitt attack, Flying Officer Gowers was lucky and descended by parachute, but his hands had been badly burned. The diary of the 472nd Light Anti Aircraft records:

"A Hurricane from the 85th Squadron attacked a hostile formation. His plane became out of control and crashed at Q733733. The wounded pilot baled out at Woldingham Heights and was treated by civil police."

Gowers landed near Chelsham. The wreck of his Hurricane was recovered by 49 MU on 26 September.

**Flying Officer
Arthur Gowers.**

Arthur Gowers had been with 85 Squadron since 1938, but had only recently become an operational pilot again after a long illness. Since the squadron had arrived at Croydon on 19 August he had shot down a Bf110 on the 30th and two Me109s on the 31st.

He recovered from his burns and by October 1943 he was squadron leader of 183 Squadron, but was shot down in his Typhoon off Cherbourg and posted 'missing'.

The 85 Squadron Hurricane of P/O A.G. Lewis was badly shot up over Kenley and he had to make a wheels-up landing after he suffered a jammed undercarriage.

Sgt. John Ellis was another of 85 Squadron's pilots that did not return to Kenley that day. He was last seen in combat with Me109s near Biggin Hill, but there was no further word of him; he was eventually posted as 'missing'.

**Sergeant
John Ellis.**

His Hurricane, P2673, was finally discovered buried beneath a field at Chelsfield, east of Biggin Hill, in 1992. This discovery led to the identification of an 'unknown' pilot, whose remains had been buried at Orpington, as the remains of John Ellis he was re-buried at Brookwood Military Cemetery.

Flight Lieutenant Lee and Flying Officer Lewis of 85 Squadron.

1 September 1940

Hurricane, L2062
79 Squadron
Location:
Hollymeoak Road, Hooley

Time: 14.08 hours
Pilot:
Pilot Officer Brian Robert Noble (24)
injured

Brian Noble went straight from training to 79 Squadron at Biggin Hill in June 1940 and shared in the destruction of an He59 float plane on 28 August. Although he baled out from his Hurricane he suffered terrible burns and became one of the famous 'Guinea Pigs' at East Grinstead Hospital. He did not return to operations, but held staff posts until he retired with the rank of Wing Commander in 1969.

All that was left of Noble's Hurricane.

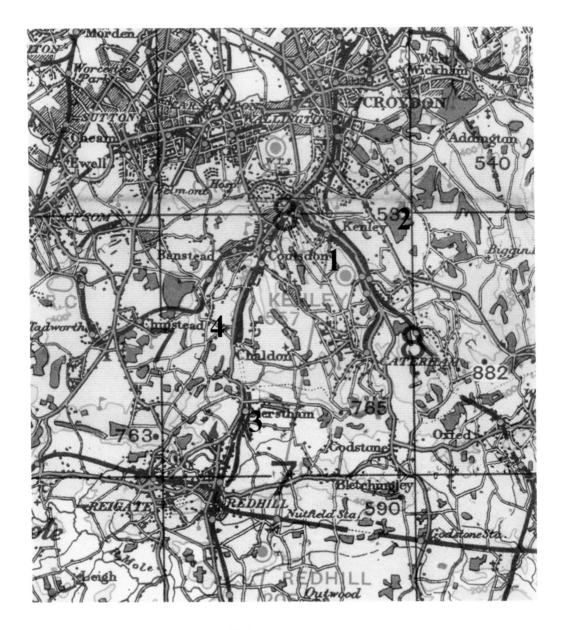

The aircraft losses on 1st September 1940

1 Flying Officer Patrick Philip Woods-Scawen - Zig-Zag Road, Kenley.

2 Sergeant Glendon Booth - Kingswood, Sanderstead.

3 Flying Officer Arthur Gowers - Merstham.

4 Pilot Officer Brian Noble - Hollymeoak Road, Hooley.

For the past two days German aircraft had not penetrated far enough inland to become involved in combat over Surrey, although the squadrons at Croydon and Kenley had been busy enough meeting the enemy high over the Kent coast.

On 4 September, in accordance with new directives from the Oberkommando der Luftwaffe to disrupt aircraft production, a large-scale attack was planned against the Vickers and Hawker aircraft factories at Brooklands, near Weybridge. Only Bf110s were to be used with no heavy bombers and no fighter escort; they would have to fight their own way to and from the target.

Thus the scene was set for two protagonists familiar in the skies of Surrey to clash, the Hurricanes of No.253 Squadron and the Messerschmitt Bf110s of Erprobungsgruppe 210.

CIRCLE OF DEATH

By September 1940, the Bf110, much vaunted 'Destroyer' of the Luftwaffe was beginning to show its weaknesses in combat. Designed and produced as a heavy fighter-bomber, it was certainly fast, heavily armed and capable of carrying a useful bomb load over a fair range. It was when it met high performance single engined fighters over France, and later England, that its lack of manoeuvrability was found to be its Achilles heel.

To counter this, the tactic of flying several aircraft in a circle was developed, the fire from both front and rear guns covering the other machines. In theory there would be no 'tail ender' for fighters to pick off and a group of Bf110s could protect each other against fighter attack.

THE MORNING'S ACTIVITY

The first signs of the day's coming activity showed on the plotting tables of Fighter Command shortly after 8.30. Seven Hurricanes of 111 Squadron had clashed with Me109s off Folkestone and lost two men.

During the next half an hour plots of enemy aircraft were received from Observer Corps throughout South Eastern England. The plots were random, no obvious pattern or objective could be discerned, and no attacks were heading for the airfields. 11 Group's controllers began to scramble squadrons with orders to patrol their bases, just in case. There were now no less than 13 fighter squadrons in the air, yet not a single interception resulted. The plotting tables gradually emptied until, by midday, they were clear of enemy aircraft.

At Kenley 253 Squadron's day had got off to a bad start. A recently arrived pilot, Flying Officer Trueman, took off with the squadron and dived into the ground near Banstead. He was killed.

4 September 1940

Hurricane, V6638
253 Squadron
Location:
In garden of Broadview, Tudor Close, Banstead

Time: 09.45 hours

Pilot:
Pilot Officer Alec Albert Gray Trueman (26) - killed

THE MYSTERY OF THE BANSTEAD HURRICANE

The residents of Banstead, on the chalk hills to the north of Surrey had become accustomed to seeing the 'planes from Kenley and Croydon. From the high ground of the Downs, London was clearly visible to the north, lying in its basin, and on a clear day the tiny specs of aircraft could be seen moving slowly in the far distance. They were familiar too with the noise of aircraft overhead, Merlin engines of Hurricanes and Spitfires, and more recently the sound of German aircraft and of gunfire.

On this Wednesday a different sound was heard overhead, a noise that grew ever louder and rose in pitch until heads turned to search the sky for its source. For a brief few seconds some saw a Hurricane in its last moments before it disappeared behind houses in The Nork and was replaced by a rising column of dark grey smoke; only then did the sound of a dull, rumbling thud, reach their ears.

For a while chaos reigned in Tudor Close; the very earth had shaken, windows had shattered, tiles had fallen from roofs and ornaments tumbled from shelves to smash on the floor.

The crash site at Tudor Close in 1940.

As the local police cordoned off the road and military personnel arrived the story became clear, a fighter had dived vertically into a garden and exploded, there was almost nothing left of it. Still later it became clear that the unfortunate pilot had still been in the cockpit when it crashed.

News reached Kenley by telephone. A Hurricane had crashed, was it one of theirs? Alec Trueman from 253 Squadron had not returned from a flight, perhaps it was him?

66

Pilot Officer Alec Trueman.

Eventually it was established that Trueman had crashed with his Hurricane, but no enemy activity had been reported in the area. What had become of him?

There were many theories, but the most likely ones came from his fellow pilots. Alec was in the habit of closing the hood of his Hurricane before taking off and did not put on his oxygen mask until he gained height.

The two possibilities this gave rise to were either carbon monoxide poisoning, from the engine's exhaust while he was without oxygen, or anoxia, passing out through lack of oxygen supply to his mask. It seems certain that one of these technical failures led directly to his death without a shot being fired.

Canadian born Alec Trueman had trained as a Hampden bomber pilot, but re-trained as a fighter pilot at 6 OTU in June 1940, joining 253 Squadron in July. He reported that he damaged an Me109 on 2 September, but was lost in this accident two days later.

The same site at Tudor Close forty years later when the Hurricane was excavated.

THE RAID ON BROOKLANDS

As had happened that morning, the enemy was plotted assembling over France. Two small formations were now near Calais and, over Norent Fontes, a plot grew from 20 plus to an estimated 100 plus. A fourth force of 50 plus was moving south-west from Boulogne down the Channel. At 12.30 eleven squadrons were despatched to counter the new threat. The He111s continued towards their target of Gravesend.

Here 501 Squadron was barely able to get airborne before the bombs began to fall, none, however, hit the airfield itself. In fact, despite the number that had fallen in past weeks, few bombs hit the airfield.

As this combat was being fought the main formation from Norrent Fontes had been progressing down the Channel. Off Hastings a small force split away and turned inland, the remainder of the force held its course.

As the pilots of 602 Squadron engaged, the leading 110s turned anti-clockwise to form a defensive circle. 'A' Flight and Green Section went into the 110 escort, but Blue Section had lost the remainder of the squadron in the turn. No.79 Squadron's 'A' Flight from Biggin Hill patrolling the Beachy Head area at the same time found fifteen Bf110s over the sea and joined the melee.

One Messerschmitt in particular came in for attention. Four pilots attacked one Bf110 that dived straight into the sea with dense black smoke pouring from its port engine.

Whilst the main force of 110s had been flying west along the Channel, the unit that had crossed the coast near Hastings had been making its way towards Tunbridge Wells. This was a diversion mounted by II./ZG76. 72 Squadron's nine Spitfires from Croydon had been vectored south, to intercept this force. The nine were led by Red and Yellow sections in two vics with the three remaining aircraft acting as rear guard. Red and Yellow sections went into line astern formation as the enemy broke up their echelon formation to go line astern and turn into their usual defensive circle.

The first six Spitfire pilots began their attack before the circle was complete. In all, 72 Squadron's pilots claimed the destruction of three Ju86s and six Bf110s, with one damaged. An official report later stated: '3 of the Ju 86s were claimed as shot down, but no wreckage was found afterwards from which it could be confirmed that the Germans were using this obsolescent aircraft'. There were only three Bf110s brought down in this engagement.

The diversionary force ploughed its way on to drop their bombs in and around Chatham. In Rochester, Pobjoy's aircraft factory was hit but it escaped major damage. The pilots of II./ZG76 made their escape over the Thames and southern Essex to safety.

Fourteen bomb-carrying Bf110s of Erprobungsgruppe 210 with an escort of more Bf110s from V/Lehrgeschwader 1 crossed the Channel to Worthing, where they met 234 Squadron's Spitfires and the Hurricanes of 79 and 43 squadrons who were already waiting for them. Upon seeing the oncoming fighters Hauptmann Hans von Boltenstern, Gruppenkommandeur of Erprobungsgruppe 210, pushed his control column forward and put his Bf110 into a dive. Without a shot being fired the 110 crashed into the sea off Worthing. His fellow crews looked on in amazement and could only put it down to panic. The high-ranking commander had little combat experience.

Between them the RAF pilots claimed a total of no less than twenty Bf110s and one Do17 'destroyed', with seven more Bf110s damaged. In a later report it was stated: *'When the individual combat reports were examined at Fighter Command HQ all but one were allowed.'*

---

4 September 1940

Hurricane, P3676	**Time: 09.45 hours**
79 Squadron	Pilot:
Location:	**Sergeant John Wright (24)**
South of Wentworth Close, Tolworth	**killed**

On his return to Biggin Hill Sergeant Wright attempted to crash land his Hurricane near Surbiton, but crashed heavily and slid along the ground. Scotsman John Wright was lifted from his cockpit severely injured and died from his injuries in Surbiton Hospital the following day.

Like Alec Trueman, John Wright was trained at 6 OTU in June 1940 and went straight to an operational fighter squadron. He had shared in the destruction of an He111 off the north-east coast, then came south with his squadron and was lost shortly after.

Meanwhile, the Hurricane pilots of 1 (RCAF) Squadron had been heading south from their Northolt base. At 18,000 feet, when just west of Horsham, they spotted the leading group of II./ZG76's Bf110s flying 3,000 feet below them, still in their defensive circle.

Mr Waller, and his friend Mr Oliver, were in a small boat, fishing for pike in Burton Lake. Their fishing was interrupted by a commotion above them. A 110 came overhead, seemingly full of holes, pursued by a pack of Hurricanes. Shortly after a tremendous mushroom of flame and smoke rose from the direction of Pulborough. Mr Oliver turned to his friend and remarked, 'I never thought I'd live to see anything like that' and carried on fishing. The Bf110s of Erprobungsgruppe 210 were still heading north to their target of Brooklands.

Albert Hyde had worked at Vickers since 1938 until one dinnertime when he used a pair of steps to climb onto the wing of a Wellington to inspect the landing lamps. Someone moved the steps and he fell heavily, injuring his head. The wound had still not healed completely when returned to the factory to see his foreman, Bert Gates, about coming back. A date having been set for his return, Albert got onto a bus and left Brooklands at 1 o'clock.

When he reached home he could clearly see aircraft in the sunshine; and bombs falling on the workshop he had been in just 20 minutes earlier.

The time was now twenty-three minutes past one. Workers at the Vickers aircraft factory on the old Brooklands racetrack near Weybridge were beginning to gather around the entrance to the machine shop where they clocked on for the afternoon shift.

John Ellis was in the Vickers' Press Shop when the bombs fell without any warning. There was a tremendous 'din' and glass fell around him as he tried to reach the shelter of a cupboard, but when he opened the door two men were already in it and there was no room for him! Shaken, he made his way out of the workshop towards the railway station and waited until he felt it safe to return.

Walking back he passed the shelters in fields to the north and west of the factory and came upon a woman worker who had been partly buried by a bomb blast that had completely buried her friend just in front of her. He and a friend dug a little with their hands, but there was no sign of the other woman.

Another bomb had fallen on Shelter No.13 and blocked the entrance to No.14, but these shelters were further north and fortunately no one had time to reach them. His nerves were shaken and he was off work till Christmas.

Bill Hayes, a senior aircraft inspector, and his colleague Tug Wilson had gone outside to escape the heat in the canteen when the first bombs fell.

"I was dazed and bleeding. I tried to get up on my feet and was almost on my knees when two more bombs fell at the front of the building known as the Archie Knight repair hangar, only 50 yards away. Suddenly the air became like night, full of black dust and smoke. I realised the position I was in and knew that if I could get between the sand bags and the outer wall of the machine shop I might be safe from further bombs. I ran around the corner and flung myself down between the sandbags and the wall. Somehow I had become separated from Tug because when I looked round I couldn't see him anywhere.

"I saw another chap trying to get away from where he was laying - he kept shouting, 'I want to get out, I want to get out!' I grabbed hold of him and held him down just as one of the diving planes started machine-gunning. The bullets zig-zagged across the concrete, just missing the feet of the man I was holding down. I hung on to him as long as I could, but he suddenly got free and the last I saw of him he was running in the direction of Weybridge with lumps of rock and concrete falling all around him. After that I tried to get up but found that part of the sliding doors had fallen over me. I pulled myself out from underneath."

Bill Hayes then went into the machine shop.

"My first sight was that of the bodies of two men I knew who had been outside with me just before the bombing. The first was lying dead beside my desk and was a terrible sight. The other had been crushed between the fuselages of two Wellingtons which had been blown together by the blast."

(This account first appeared in Howard Johnson's book Wings over Brooklands.)

Tragedy struck the Coleman family when four were killed. The bodies of the mother, father and son were found, but the body of their seventeen-year-old daughter was never recovered.

The fourteen aircraft of Erprobungsgruppe 210 had dived down onto the airfield, dropping 28, 500kg bombs. A single bomb had caused most of the casualties. It fell on the Vickers machine shop, went through the roof and a light reinforced concrete first floor before penetrating ten feet below the machine shop floor. The blast from the explosion collapsed the first floor and roof. Pieces of metal, tools, concrete and general paraphernalia of a workshop scythed through the air, killing many of the workers sitting in the shop during their dinner break.

One identified but unclaimed and four unidentified bodies were buried at the Council's Burvale Cemetery at 2.30 p.m. on Monday the 9th September.

The damage and loss of life at the Vickers plant at Brooklands was a bitter blow. The damage was caused by a single bomb that had found its target. The loss of production was estimated to be equivalent to two months' output; that is 24 Wellingtons. The Hawker assembly shops producing Hurricanes had not been hit.

The effect upon the morale of the staff seemed at first to be serious. The report stated that *'there was a great feeling of resentment not against the enemy but the authority who failed to warn them, and the soldiers manning the Bofors guns who did nothing effective in reply'.*

It was suggested that:

1. The factory should keep a similar plot on enemy aircraft movement as in Fighter Command HQ.

2. Lookouts should be on roofs or in a circle around the factory with telephone connections.

3, Last minute warnings should be passed from Fighter Command through the local gun defence organisation.

"Most of all the workforce wanted to know why there were no gun crews standing by and why when the Bofors opened fire they did so with a range and accuracy which would have been laughable if the circumstances had not been so tragic.

'Despite this the nerve of the work force as a whole was not badly shaken; indeed the women reported for duty as usual the next morning."

At 1 o'clock nine of 253 Squadron's pilots took off to patrol the Croydon area. Flight Lieutenant Cambridge, leading the squadron, was informed of aircraft approaching from the south east, then the south west, and finally from the west. The squadron climbed into the sun and saw the attack on Brooklands in progress away to the north-west. Wheeling to starboard in a shallow vic the squadron dived on the enemy, descending from 12,000 to 6,000 feet, and attacked Erprobungsgruppe 210's escort.

---

4 September 1940

Messerschmitt Bf110D
Wn. 3303, L1+BK, 14./LG1
Location:
Broom House, Long Reach, Ockham

Time: 13.25 Hours
Crew:
Feldwebel Röhring - killed
Unteroffizier Joachim Jäckel
baled out, injured

Shot down by pilots of No.253 Squadron.

Flight Lieutenant Cambridge reported: *"I picked my target and attacked him from the beam and above. I kept firing as I closed; the port engine caught fire, the enemy did a stall turn to port and I followed him still firing. He then went into a dive and I kept on firing. I expended all my ammunition and followed him down to the ground."*

Cambridge had not been alone in this attack. Pilot Officer Corkett had also been attacking this 110 as it passed over the village of Ockham. Gunner, Joachim Jäckel, had been wounded by the fire and had baled out, but Feldwebel Röhring went down with his machine and was killed. Jackel landed near the village where the local doctor tended to his wounds; later one of his bloodstained flying boots was displayed at a garden fete. The money raised went towards the local 'Spitfire Fund'.

---

4 September 1940

Messerschmitt Bf110D
Wn. 3306, L1+FK, 14./LG1
Location:
Green Dene, Horsley

Time: 13.25 Hours
Crew:
Oberleutnant Michel Junge (26) - killed
Unteroffizier Karl Bremser (25) - killed

Shot down by pilots of No.253 Squadron.

Flight Lieutenant Wedgewood was leading Red Section and attacked the rear formation of 110s: *"I got on to the tail of a Jaguar (110) and started firing at about 250 yards and closed to point blank range, the enemy caught fire, climbed steeply for a second and then crashed into a wood."*

Sergeant Dredge had made the attack with Wedgewood and closed from 30 to 25 yards; he saw both engines and the cockpit on fire before L1+FK exploded at Green Dene.

Two other 253 Squadron pilots claimed aircraft destroyed, Pilot Officer Samolinski and Pilot Officer Nowak, whilst Sergeant Kee only claimed to have damaged his victim. In all six aircraft were claimed as destroyed, but only two aircraft fell as a result of this combat.

The Bf110 crews now had a few minutes peace as the jubilant pilots of 253 Squadron returned to Kenley. As they fled south to the coast more fighters were preparing to meet them, again over Worthing.

The combats that developed during this day were complicated, but no more so than many of the Battle of Britain or other conflicts. In such a fast moving battle things soon became confused, and naturally so, leading to many distorted reports.

Fighter Command claims for enemy aircraft brought down during the Brooklands raid and associated diversions were:

34 Bf110s destroyed, 14 damaged and 4 probables

3 Do17s

3 Ju86s

In France the band played on - under the wing of a Bf110 from Erprobungsgruppe 210.

a single Me109 destroyed

...from an estimated total of 100 aircraft employed.

Over 65 years later it seems that a figure of fifteen Bf110s destroyed would be more realistic. Erprobungsgruppe 210 escaped without loss, but they had not yet finished with Brooklands.

6TH SEPTEMBER 1940

6 September 1940

Messerschmitt Bf110C-4
Wn. 2146, U8+CL, 3/ZG26
Location:
Old Coulsdon Golf Course, Coulsdon
Time: 09.33 Hours

Crew:
Unteroffizier Christoph Kiehn (27)
killed
Unteroffizier Egon Neusz (20)
injured, PoW

Shot down by Hurricanes

The action in the skies of Surrey began early in the morning when a formation of Bf110s was again taken on by Hurricanes near Croydon and Kenley. This time a Bf110 of 3./Zerstorergeschwader 26 was brought down by the Hurricanes. Gustav Kiehn found himself embroiled in a fight and machine-gun bullets struck his aircraft; his gunner, Egon Neusz, was hit by a bullet in a hand.

As he tried to break away and flee for home there was an explosion and his Bf110 went into a spin, which was when the gunner decided his best course of action was to bale out, but he only just managed it and got out at 800 feet, moments before the aircraft crashed and exploded.

One of the Hurricane pilots, Sergeant Tweed, was forced to bale out of his aircraft over Woldingham after it was hit by gunfire. He suffered a bullet wound to one knee, but was otherwise unhurt.

Dennis Knight's sketch showing the last moments of U8+CL

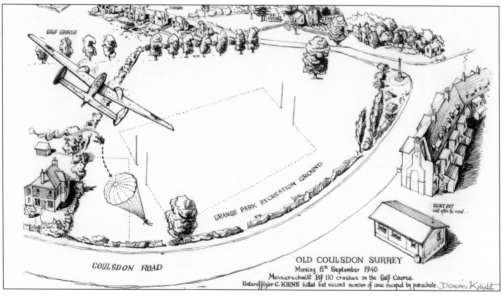

The crash site at Coulsdon shortly after the Bf110 fell to earth.

In an attempt to complete the destruction of the aircraft works at Brooklands, the Bf110s of Erprobungsgruppe 210 returned to Surrey once again. The raid was a repeat of the effort of September 4th, when the escort fighters sustained heavy losses, but this time the escort escaped unscathed and Erprobungsgruppe 210 was intercepted by fighters and little damage was done to Brooklands.

The Messerschmitts had taken off from Calais-Marck and flown to Cap Gris Nez where they climbed for 14 minutes before setting a course of 298 degrees for Kenley, from where Brooklands was only two minutes flying time. After the attack they were to head on a bearing of 132 degrees for 28 minutes, that would bring them back over Boulogne and safety.

They reached their target without hindrance and would probably have had no casualties had it not been for a problem with the Hurricane flown by Pilot Officer Dibnah of No.1 Squadron. Dibnah's propeller had been giving him trouble and he broke away from his formation to return to his airfield, but he then saw a group of enemy aircraft heading for the coast and, alone, decided to make an attack. On his first attack his target climbed and turned, giving him a chance of a head-on pass; theBf110 turned and a man baled out, then it began a spiral dive into the ground near Oxted where it exploded.

Messerschmitt Bf110D-0
Wn. 3373, S9+BH, 1/EprG 210
Location:
Foyles Farm, Crowhurst

Time: 09.25 Hours
Crew:
Unteroffizier Gerhard Rüger (24) - killed
Gefreiter Edmund Ernst (20) - PoW

Shot down by Pilot Officer Dibnah of No.1 Squadron

Twenty-year-old Edmund Ernst escaped from his rear cockpit and parachuted safely down to earth near south Bletchingly tunnel, where Canadian troops took him in to custody. Gerhard Rüger did not get out. Perhaps he had been incapacitated by the gunfire from the Hurricane, but for some reason he was still in his cockpit when the Bf110 hit the ground at great speed. It then cart-wheeled across a field, disintegrating as it went, and finally exploded in a sheet of flame some 200 yards long. According to eyewitnesses interviewed by Dennis Knight in the 1960s, Rüger's body was found in a burning haystack and buried by fireman and Canadian soldiers in a makeshift grave near the crash site where he lies to this day. *(right)*.

Hurricane, L1892
111 Squadron
Location:
Beddlestead Farm, Woldingham

Time: 09.00 hours
Pilot:
Sergeant Leslie John Tweed (19)
injured

Leslie Tweed joined the RAF Volunteer Reserve in August 1939 and was called up a few days later when war was declared. After basic training he was posted to 111 Squadron on 27 July 1940, but was not considered to be competent to fly in combat and sent for further training to 6 OTU, returning to the squadron on 24 August.

On 6 September he shared in the destruction of an enemy aircraft at 20,000 feet, but was then shot down by return fire. He lost consciousness before he could bale out, but fortunately recovered just in time to get out at only 1,200 feet. He landed by parachute and lost consciousness once again. He did not fly in combat again, but survived the war and stayed in the RAF until retirement in 1972.

The bright skies over southern England remained largely clear of enemy aircraft until the late afternoon, when around 350 raiders began a massed attack on east and south-east London. The Surrey based squadrons were among the fighters sent to meet the threat along with pilots from further afield. Among them was Caesar Hull, leading the Hurricanes of 43 Squadron from Tangmere in Sussex. 27 RAF fighters were lost this day, but only one fell in Surrey.

---

7 September 1940

Hurricane, V6641
43 Squadron
Location:
Boys County School,
Old Coulsdon

Time: 16.45 hours
Pilot:
Squadron Leader Caesar Barraud Hull
DFC (27)
killed

Shot down by fire from Me109s

Born in Southern Rhodesia, his privileged background led him to the Springbok boxing team that visited England for the 1934 Empire Games.

After initial training with the South African Air Force he was forced to seek a career in the RAF as he did not speak Afrikaans and joined 43 Squadron in 1936. He became a flight commander with the ill-fated 263 Squadron's expedition to Norway, during which he was shot down and injured, but returned to England to recover.

Flight Lieutenants Peter Townsend and (right) Caesar Hull.

He re-joined 43 Squadron the day after the Squadron Leader's death on 30 August and assumed command of the squadron; a command that lasted just one week. On 7 September he led the squadron towards south London to intercept a raid of Dornier 17s escorted by Me109s and is believed to have fallen victim to a roving fighter pilot.

On this day the Luftwaffe's commanders chose to hold back their main attack until the late afternoon. At around 6 o'clock a large force including 26 Heinkel He111s with a similar number of Bf110s and as many as 60 Me109 escorts was making its way across north Surrey, passing over Kenley and heading west towards Farnborough. Climbing to meet them were 70 RAF fighters from nine squadrons including, for the first time, the 'Duxford Wing' from far to the north of London. With time to get into formation the squadrons, led by the legendary legless pilot Douglas Bader, took the Luftwaffe pilots by surprise; the RAF, they had been told, was on its knees; not able to put up such a formidable display of force.

Over Croydon, the two forces clashed. With such a large number of aircraft in one place the combat instantly became confused in a mêlée of turning, climbing and diving aircraft. Some formations split up and fled south, Bf110s went into their familiar defensive circle and deserted the Heinkel bombers they should have been protecting.

From No.310 Squadron, part of the Duxford Wing, two Hurricane pilots made to attack the same Messerschmitt, unaware of each other's presence. The two aircraft collided. Now out of control, one of the Hurricanes collided with a Bf110 and all three machines began to fall from the sky over Woodmanstern.

The crash of Boulton's Hurricane recorded by Dennis Knight.

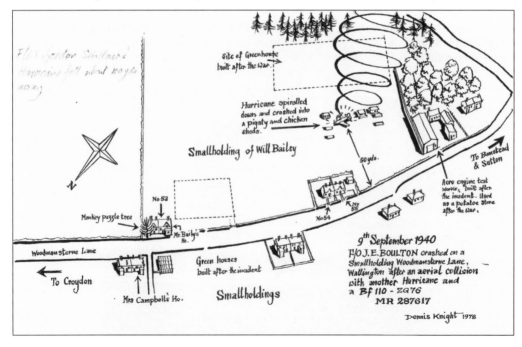

HISTORIAN DENNIS KNIGHT WITNESSED THE EVENT AND LATER IDENTIFIED THE PILOTS INVOLVED:

"Two Hurricanes dived simultaneously onto the raider. The fighters collided; Sinclair had a wing folded up on his Hurricane by the impact. Boulton's fighter flew into the Messerschmitt and locked itself onto the raider's twin finned tailplane. The Messerschmitt's nose reared up as the weight of the falling Hurricane started to drag it down tail first. Turning onto its back the bomber allowed the Hurricane to work free and start its own spin to destruction. The sky was filled with tiny pieces from both aircraft.

The bomber, with its tail bent over at an angle, put its nose down and started its own spin to earth. As the Messerschmitt went down it spun flashing light and dark in the sun, and emitting white smoke and vapour. Two parachutes opened high in the blue haze. The bomber went into the ground with an explosion that rocked the houses. Its motors were forced some ten feet down into the solid chalk.

Mr and Mrs Stacey were living at a house called Kennicott at the time, but only Mrs Stacey with a companion Mrs Saunders were at home.

During the raid they had both gone into the drawing room and sat nursing a cat and dog behind closed curtains. They both heard the sound of the falling bomber getting louder and louder as its screaming motors assisted its descent.

Then there was a terrific crash. Both sat still for seconds then, walking to the back of the house and drawing the curtains they saw a great column of black smoke and wreckage all over the garden. Ammunition began to explode and shrapnel and bullets began to break the windows.

Mr and Mrs Hallan were very fortunate; they were in the shelter at the bottom of their garden and only just escaped being incinerated in their shelter.

By now dozens of people began to arrive with Police, Home Guard, Fire Brigade and soon the area was cordoned off and the sightseers hustled away. The fire was brought under control. Troops guarded the wreckage for several days while the Council tried to recover the remains of the crew. A pistol was found, a watch and a few remains of an airman, later identified as W Zimmermann.

The other member of the crew, Feldwebel L Ostermüncher, jumped as the Messerschmitt fell. His canopy opened with a crack close by his falling aircraft. It caught, ripped, and sent him hurtling to earth. His boots had jerked off when his parachute opened and he lay bare footed in a field for some three days while a dispute was settled as to which authority was responsible for his removal."

It was reported by RAF Air Intelligence that the body also had a bullet wound near the heart. Finally Frank Payne of Carshalton removed him and buried him in All Saints Parish Church, Carshalton. In later years an old lady began to tend the lone grave when it became neglected, but threats from other women frightened her and she too let it become overgrown.

Dennis Knight.

During the late afternoon 9th September, an extraordinary multiple collision occurred over Coulsdon, Surrey. The above is a faithful record of the incident seen by myself from the gardens of "Danton" No 8 Woodcote Grove Road, Coulsdon, opposite St. Andrew's Church.

Research into the affair revealed that two Hurricanes of No 310 sqdn. Collided, one British pilot then rammed a German aircraft (described in records as a Dornier, but in fact an Me 110).

However, I certainly saw four fighters spin away at the same moment exactly as shown above. Subsequent research established that two other Hurricanes both of No 242 sqdn did crash nearby at the same time! One fell at old Coulsdon and the other in Caterham Valley. The lone Hurricane seen climbing above the falling aircraft was flown by S/ldr Douglas Bader.

80

9 September 1940

Hurricane, V7412
310 Squadron
Location:
Woodmanstern Lane, Woodmanstern

Time: 17.35 hours
Pilot:
Flying Officer John Eric Boulton (20) killed

Collided with the Hurricane flown by Gordon Sinclair

---

9 September 1940

Hurricane, R4084
310 Squadron
Location:
Woodmanstern Lane, Woodmanstern

Time: 17.35 hours
Pilot:
Flight Lieutenant Gordon Leonard Sinclair (24) - baled out safely

Collided with the Hurricane flown by Boulton

---

9 September 1940

Messerschmitt Bf110C
Wn. 3207, 2N+EP, 9./ZG76

Location:
Woodcote Park Avenue, Woodmanstern

Time: 17.35 Hours
Crew:
Leutnant Eduard Ostermüncher (24) baled out but killed
Gefreiter Werner Zimmermann (20) killed

Collided with the Hurricane flown by Flying Officer Boulton

Boulton, trapped in his Hurricane, died when it fell onto a pigsty in Woodmanstern Lane and burst into flames, killing several of the pigs. He was originally buried at Bandon Hill Cemetery as an unknown RAF pilot. Sinclair managed to extricate himself from his machine and parachuted down onto the Purley Way with a sprained ankle.

John Boulton was a pre-war flying instructor and attached to the Czech 310 Squadron in July to checkout and help the new pilots arriving at the squadron. When the squadron became operational in August he sought permission from the Air Ministry to fly operationally, which was finally granted. He shared in the shooting down of an He111 on 7 September, but was killed in the collision two days later.

Gordon Sinclair had a successful career with 19 Squadron in the early days of the battle, but was posted to the new 310 Squadron as 'A' Flight Commander. When his new squadron became operational he continued his earlier successes until the collision. He sustained a sprained ankle and returned to combat only to be shot down on 29 September when he again baled out. He retired from the RAF in 1957 as a Wing Commander.

John Boulton and
Gordon Sinclair
(centre) with
the pilots of
310 Squadron.

The combat sprawled southwards as the bomber and escorts fled south. Over Kenley an Me109 pilot brought the Hurricane of Pilot Officer Sclanders down in flames; the pilot did not get out. Return fire from a Bf110 or a Dornier hit Sergeant Lonsdale's Hurricane and he was forced to take to his parachute. As he floated down his machine dived into a road just outside of the airfield's boundary and burst a water main. After chasing the retreating enemy southwards Czech pilot, Pilot Officer Rypl ran short of fuel and was obliged to land his Hurricane at Limpsfield. The aircraft was slightly damaged and lay in a field for a week until it was dismantled and taken for repair. Rypl was able to walk away and re-joined his squadron.

---

9 September 1940

Hurricane, P3142	**Time: 17.35 hours**
310 Squadron	Pilot:
Location:	**Flight Lieutenant Frantisek Rypl**
Rough Wood, Limpsfield	**safe**

Force landed in a field when short of fuel after combat with Me109s and hit a fence. Aircraft repairable.

Frantisek Rypl had left his native Czechoslovakia for Poland when his country had been annexed by Germany and flew with a Czech squadron in Poland; then left Poland for Britain where he was posted to the newly formed 310 Squadron. Nothing is known of his career after the Battle of Britain, but he did return to Czechoslovakia after the war.

Boulton, Jerrard Jeffries DFC and Sinclair pose for the camera just days before the collision over Woodmanstern.

---

09 September 1940

Hurricane, P2831
242 Squadron
Location:
Ninehams Road, Kenley

Time: 17.45 hours
Pilot:
Sergeant Robert Henry Lonsdale baled out safely

Shot down by return fire.

Robert Lonsdale had escaped from Norway in June when most of his squadron had been killed in the sinking of HMS Glorious. He was posted to 242 Squadron and shot down an He111 on 30 August and claimed another enemy aircraft on 9 September, but his Hurricane was damaged by return fire and he baled out. Later in the war he became an instructor in Canada and finally re-trained as a Lancaster pilot flying with Bomber Command.

---

09 September 1940

Hurricane, P3087
242 Squadron
Location: **Near the railway viaduct, Woldingham Road, Caterham**

Time: 17.45 hours
Pilot:
Pilot Officer Kirkpatrick MacLure Sclanders (24) - killed

Shot down by return fire from Bf110s.

Canadian Sclanders was desperate to fly in combat. He had actually learnt to fly at just 15 years of age, but had to wait until his seventeenth birthday to be granted a licence. As part of a travelling airshow he played the part of a boy scout who accidentally started a 'plane's engine; and then flew a stunt routine. In 1935 he came

to England and joined the RAF, but returned to Canada with a serious illness that prevented his joining the RCAF after his recovery.

Frustrated, Sclanders tried to fly in the Russo-Finnish war, but it was over before he could see action, so he attempted to join the French Air Force, only to be forced to flee the advancing German forces in 1940.

Thus he arrived back in Britain, and once again joined the RAF. After training on Hurricanes he was posted to 242 Squadron on 26 August, but shot down and killed twelve days later.

A painting by Mark Postlethwaite depicting Douglas Bader leading 242 Squadron alongside 310 Squadron in a scramble from Duxford as he did on this day.

Messerschmitt Bf110C-4
L1+DL, Wn. 3298, 15./LG1
Location:
Sports Ground, Old Malden Lane,
Worcester Park

Time: 18.00 Hours
Crew:
Unteroffizier Otto Kramp(25)
Unteroffizier A Pfaffelhuber (25)
both killed

Shot down by Hurricanes

Otto Kramp had been flying Bf110s with Lehrgeschwader 1 since May 1940, and flying escort missions to bomb-carrying Bf110s since August. In the past six weeks he had seen a lot of combat and recorded the details in a small diary:

24 August	Escorting bomber formation.
25 August	Escorting bomber formation. Attacked by Hurricane near Portland. 38 shots in starboard engine and steering gear. Bullet through tyre.
26 August	Escorting bomber formation. Twice attacked by Spitfires, 30km east of Portland. One Spitfire shot down by Bf110 astern of us.
29 August	Freelance patrol to South London. Saw only a few enemy fighters.
30 August	Escorting He111 formation to Aldershot. One Hurricane shot down 12.20 hrs 15 km north of Rye. One Hurricane shot down 12.23 hrs 10 km west of Rye.
30 August	Escorting bomber formation to Radlett. Attacked two Hurricanes and one Spitfire. Forced to land at St Omer owing to lack of petrol.
1 September	Escorting bomber formation to south-east London. W/T operator shot down Hurricane.
2 September	War Flight.
4 September	Escorting 14 Bf110 bombers to Vickers Wellington works, Aldershot. There were about 30 enemy aircraft (Latest type Bristol, probably American). Violent air fighting at Aldershot, and we retired.
6 September	Escorting Bf110 bombers to Vickers Wellington works at Aldershot. Saw five enemy fighters, but no fighting.
7 September	Escorting bomber Geschwader to London. Fifteen enemy fighters. Attacked twice by Spitfires. Escaped by doing spiral turn and shot at one of the Spitfires.
8 September	Escorting bomber Geschwader to London. Slight contact with enemy. Three Spitfires. Two Me109s collided in mid air. AA scored direct hit on Do17. Counted seven parachutes.

9 September 1940 was to be Otto's thirteenth raid over England. Clearly he was no stranger to Surrey's skies, for he had already been involved in the fighting of 30 August, and had escorted Erprobungsgruppe 210 on the 4 September and 6 September Brooklands raids (although he believed the target to be Aldershot). Now he was taking off from Ligescourt; escorting the bombers again with his gunner and radio operator Pfaffelhuber behind him.

The air combat that evening, high over Tolworth, was witnessed by many. Bombs had fallen nearby and around the railway lines near Surbiton; cheers went up as fighters got the better of a twin-engined 'Hun' and he started down in a steep dive with smoke pouring behind it. A terrific explosion sent flames and black oily smoke into the sky over the sports ground known as 'The Maori Club', acting as a beacon for young boys to aim their bicycles towards in their search for much treasured souvenirs. Some found their twisted metal or rubber parts to be proudly shown to friends, yet others, not quick enough to beat the police and ARP wardens, were turned away empty handed.

RAF Air Intelligence Officers searching the wreckage of the Messerschmitt found parts of a letter D, painted in yellow with a red border, and an envelope marked with the Feldpostnummer (field post number) that corresponded to the 5th Gruppe of Lehrgeschwader 1. A small diary was also found, recording twelve previous flights over England.

THE MYSTERY OF THE THIRD MAN

Parts of a body were taken away to the mortuary, where attendants determined that there were not the remains of one, but three men. The deaths were registered on 15 September as two unidentified males and D R K Helferin. Although the attendants had done their best, they had bizarrely named remains Deutscher Roter Kreuz Helferin (literally German Red Cross Helper), aged 23 of the German Air Force.

The remains were duly laid to rest in Surbiton Cemetery in grave No.5786 where the names of Kramp and Pfaffelhuber were later added to a simple wooden cross. Under the two names was inscribed 'Unknown. German Air Force. 9/9/40'.

In the late 1960s the remains were exhumed to be re-interred at the German Military Cemetery at Cannock Chase, where the mysterious and erroneous third name was finally, and correctly, deleted from the records.

The original graves of the Bf110 crew at Surbiton Cemetery.

86

SURBITON MAN WINS GEORGE MEDAL
CITATION
LEONARD MATTHEWS, LEADER ARP STRETCHER PARTY, SURBITON

"Immediately after the dropping of high explosive bombs it was learned that a man was trapped beneath the wreckage of two houses. He was located as being underneath debris immediately adjoining the party wall of another house which was in immediate danger of collapse and was, in fact, slightly moving the whole of the time that the following rescue operations were carried out.

"Matthews forced an entry through the base of the debris and dug for himself a tunnel by which to reach the trapped man.

"Having made contact with the man he then proceeded to prop up the debris from the underside, gradually making a chamber large enough for him to move the man.

"He then propped up the tunnel by which he had entered and was successful in getting the man to safety. During the whole of this time Matthews' own life was in very considerable danger, for it was impossible to shore up the collapsing adjoining wall as the strain would have been taken by the debris under which he was working.

"Throughout the whole operation Matthews proceeded in a cool, calm and efficient manner, and apart from the fact that he saved this man's life he set a brilliant example to the members of the other ARP services engaged in the locality."

The London Gazette
Tuesday 17th December 1940

11TH SEPTEMBER 1940

By early September the bombing campaign had escalated and the Luftwaffe was attacking the London Docklands by day and night. The restrictions against crews attacking London that were in force during August were a thing of the past; this was total war. As the large, slow and unwieldy bomber fleets headed for London the Hurricanes and Spitfires had time to oppose them in strength. The huge, sprawling, dogfights for which the Battle of Britain has become best known were now taking place over London itself.

---

11 September 1940

Heinkel He111H-3
Wn. 3157, 1H+ML, 3/KG26

Location:
New Barn Farm, Lingfield

Time: 16.15 Hours

Crew:
Oberleutnant Wolf Abendhausen (23) (Pilot) - PoW
Feldwebel Heinrich Westphalen (28) (Observer) - baled out, killed
Unteroffizier Hans Hauswald (21) (WT) - injured, PoW
Gefreiter Fritz Zähle (22) (mechanic) killed
Unteroffizier Bruno Herms (23) (gunner) killed

Shot down by anti-aircraft fire and fighters

Twenty-three year old bomber pilot Wolf Abendhausen and his crew were based at Wevelghem, and had paraded before Hermann Goering the previous day when he visited to present awards and promotions. Like all the men Wolf had already had a rough time at the hands of the British defences, but he had always got back.

At four o'clock he was over the docklands again when an accurate anti-aircraft shell exploded close by and put holes in one wing. His Heinkel with the letters 1H+ML painted on its fuselage and under the wings was a veteran also, with colourful yellow propeller spinners, a large yellow 'M' and a yellow band painted around its nose, all signifying the third Staffel of his Gruppe.

Things were not going well this afternoon. Despite pushing the two Junkers Jumo engines as hard as he could, Wolf could not keep up with the rest of his formation as it headed south from London, he was lagging behind the protection afforded by the large formation. Like a wounded animal the Heinkel could fall prey to fighters at any moment.

Over Lingfield the fighters struck in force. Hurricane and Spitfire pilots fell on the easy prey and shot through the engine cooling systems; eventually both engines overheated and stopped. Wolf gave orders to abandon the aircraft and he, with wireless operator Hans Hauswald, baled out. The observer, 28-year-old Heinrich

Westphalen also got out, but his parachute caught on the bomber and he was dragged down with it for a while before his parachute ripped and he fell to earth at Lingfield Lodge Farm. The Heinkel hit the ground a glancing blow and disintegrated over several fields where the bodies of the other two men were later found.

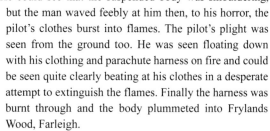

11 September 1940

Spitfire IIA, P7298
611 Squadron
Location:
49-51 Hartland Way,
Shirley

Time: 15.52 hours
Pilot:
Sergeant Frederick Ernest Richard
Shepherd (22)
baled out, killed

Landed at Frylands Wood, Farleigh. Parachute fell at Beech Farm, Slines Green.

Fighters from many airfields made for London. The Spitfires of the Duxford Wing were again in action, having had time to fly from Duxford near Cambridge to London. Pilot Officer Christopher 'Bunny' Currant was up in his 605 Squadron Hurricane from Croydon, when he witnessed the horrific death of one of the Big Wing's pilots.

At 6,000 feet, when just east of Croydon, he saw a pilot descending by parachute and decided to circle him to protect the hapless man from any German that might take a pot shot at him. He could see that the suspended body was smouldering,

but the man waved feebly at him then, to his horror, the pilot's clothes burst into flames. The pilot's plight was seen from the ground too. He was seen floating down with his clothing and parachute harness on fire and could be seen quite clearly beating at his clothes in a desperate attempt to extinguish the flames. Finally the harness was burnt through and the body plummeted into Frylands Wood, Farleigh.

Would-be rescuers searched in the wood frantically, but it was fifteen minutes before the badly burnt body was found. One man opened a tunic pocket in an effort to find some form of identification; he found some technical notes for aircraft, and a receipt for an engagement ring.

At the same time reports were coming in to the ARP Centre that a Spitfire had exploded in the air over Hartland Way, Shirley. Another tragedy then began to unfold. The largest part of the wreck, with the fuel tanks, had fallen into the garden of No.51 where Mrs Weston had taken shelter with a friend and two children. Blazing fuel started to run into the dug-out shelter and trapped them. When rescuers arrived all four were suffering from terrible burns, from which all subsequently died in hospital.

Shepherd was one of the many men who joined the RAF pre-war as ground crew, but later trained to become a pilot. In August 1940 he had completed his initial training and was posted to 611 Squadron to fly Spitfires; with little experience he was immediately sent to an Operational Training Unit to learn his new trade. He returned to his squadron on 1 September, ran out of fuel and crash-landed on 9 September, and fell in flames in tragic circumstances on 11 September.

---

11 September 1940

Hurricane, P5200	**Time: 16.09 hours**
501 Squadron	Pilot:
Location:	**Sergeant Tony Garforth Pickering (20)**
Happy Valley, Old Coulsdon	**baled out safely**

Tony Pickering had been posted straight from a Flying Training School to 32 Squadron at Biggin Hill in July 1940 along with two other inexperienced pilots, but the commanding officer saw that there was no place for them in an operational squadron and immediately sent them for further training. All three men arrived back at the squadron just as it was sent north for a rest, so they were sent on to 501 Squadron at Gravesend on 28 August.

Two weeks later Tony was shot down by Me109s near Kenley and was fortunate to bale out safely; he survived the war, leaving the RAF in 1945 as a Squadron Leader.

---

11 September 1940

Spitfire IIA, P7321	**Time: 15.55 hours**
611 Squadron	Pilot:
Location:	**Sergeant Stephen Austin Levenson**
Pendell Court, Bletchingley	**safe**

On one of his first operational sorties, Austin Levenson's Spitfire was hit by return fire from bombers he had attacked. He made a forced landing with a dead engine, but saved his aircraft from serious damage. He shot down a Dornier on 15 September and was then sent to become an instructor. He was killed over Belgium in 1942 when his Stirling bomber was shot down.

Now known as 'Battle of Britain Day' when a 'final' all-out assault was ordered by Goering and an almost continuous stream of aircraft made for London throughout the day. Every fighter squadron available was thrown against the attackers from airfields as far away as Dorset and Cambridgeshire.

---

15 September 1940

Spitfire IIA, R6609	Time: 12.30 hours
609 Squadron	Pilot:
Location:	**Pilot Officer Geoffrey Norman Gaunt (24)**
Still's Farm, Addington Village	**killed**

Broke-up in the air, one piece of a wing fell at Shirley.

It was a Spitfire based at Warmwell in Dorset that, despite the number of combats fought that day, became the only aircraft to fall in the county of Surrey. Pilot Officer Gaunt was flying one of No.609 Squadron's thirteen Spitfires that engaged the Dorniers flying over London when, it is said, he was hit in the head by a cannon shell and killed instantly. The Spitfire, now left to it own devices, broke up in the air with one piece of a wing falling at Shirley and the main wreck spinning to the ground near Addington where it was consumed by fire.

Shortly after an Me109 was seen falling just over the border into Kent. Its pilot, Oberleutnant Haase of 3./JG53, baled out but his parachute failed. His aircraft fell at Norheads Farm, west of Biggin Hill.

Yorkshireman Geoffrey Gaunt had been in the RAF as a mechanic, but on the outbreak of war was offered the chance to re-train as a pilot. Now a Spitfire pilot, he went back to his old squadron and was in combat on 25 August when he shared in the shooting down of an He111, but he fell in combat three weeks later.

**Pilot Officer
Geoffrey Gaunt.**

**The pilots of
609 Squadron
at Middle Wallop
in 1940.**

19TH/20TH SEPTEMBER 1940

As if to signal a conclusion to the battle, the Luftwaffe activity was much reduced after September 15th. The attackers had been surprised by the resilience of the RAF defenders, but they had not been beaten, a change of tactics was called for... .

Shortly after midnight a house opposite Nelson Hospital in Merton ceased to exist. Many houses had been damaged or destroyed in the past few weeks, but this one was different – it had simply disappeared, not one brick was left standing on another. This was no bomb, but the bomber itself! There was only a single civilian casualty; 25 year-old Mary Butcher, who died from her injuries six days later.

One German airman was soon captured after he landed by parachute and was immediately sent for interrogation by the RAF's Air Intelligence 'K' department that dealt with enemy airmen. By the following afternoon Squadron Leader Felkin's remarkably efficient department issued A.I.1.(k) Report No. 587/1940.

All that was left of the houses in Richmond Avenue.

---

20 September 1940

Junkers Ju88A-1
Wn. 4148, B3+HM, 4/KG54
Location:
Richmond Avenue, Merton

Time: 00.20 Hours

Crew:
Oberfeldwebel Max Röhrig (pilot) - killed
Feldwebel Hermann Fischer (observer) killed
Gefreiter K. Neumann (radio operator) killed
Feldwebel Wilhelm Schlake (28) (mechanic) - baled out, PoW

The houses were totally destroyed and replaced after the war with two houses of a more modern design.

A.I.1.(k) Report No. 587/1940.

AIR ...
20 SEP 940
TIME 23.05
3 PSD

THE FOLLOWING INFORMATION HAS BEEN OBTAINED FROM PRISONERS
OF WAR.   AS THE STATEMENTS MADE HAVE NOT AS YET BEEN VERI-
FIED, NO MENTION OF THEM SHOULD BE MADE IN INTELLIGENCE
SUMMARIES OF COMMANDS OR LOWER FORMATIONS, NOR SHOULD THEY
BE ACCEPTED AS FACTS UNTIL COMMENTED ON IN AIR MINISTRY
INTELLIGENCE SUMMARIES OR SPECIAL COMMUNICATIONS.

PLACE, DATE and TIME: Nelson Hospital, Kingston Road, Merton.
                        20.9.40.   0020 hours.

TYPE and MARKS: Ju.88.   B3 + HM   ('H' White).

UNIT: 4/K.G.54.

IDENTITY DISC: 2) 60027
                   1) 60028

FELDPOSTNUMMER: L 04785.

AUSWEIS: Grey - issued at Gütersloh 15.1.40.

START and MISSION: Started from an aerodrome N.W. of Paris at
                    2115 hours.   Mission unspecified.

- - - - - - - -

        Before starting they had been told that the weather at
16,000 feet would be favourable, but in fact it was very much worse.

        Before reaching their target, and flying at 16,000 feet, for
no apparent reason the aircraft suddenly started to dive.

        The one survivor did not know of any hits by A.A. or other
phenomena to account for this.

        The pilot regained control, but the aircraft dived again and the
Observer ordered the crew to bale out.   He baled first and does not
know what happened to the remainder of the crew.

        The aircraft crashed onto a house and there was a heavy explosion.
It is believed that the other members of the crew remained in the aircraft,
but so far only the fingers of two different bodies have been recovered.
There is no trace of the third man.

        One of the Identity Discs although it had the number stamped on
it had previously been stamped 2F/Aufkl.Gr.121.

- - - - - - - -

MORALE: Survivor fairly good.

CREW:
        Pilot........Oberfeldwebel Max RÖHRIG......... Probably dead.
        Observer.....Feldwebel Hermann FISCHER........ Probably dead.
        W/T.........Gefreiter NEUMANN................Probably dead.
        B/M.........Feldwebel Wilhelm SCHLAKE..28..(6) Slightly wounded.

A.I.1.(k).
20. 9. 40.

                                        S. D. Felkin,
                            for   Squadron Leader.

GEORGE CROSS AWARDED FOR ACTION AT BROOKLANDS.

On the morning of 21st September 1940 at about 08.30 hours the Vickers Aircraft Factory at Weybridge was attacked by an enemy aircraft.

Three bombs were dropped, two of which exploded, doing slight damage. The other, a 500-lb. bomb, penetrated the factory roof, passed through a wall at the end and came to rest on the concrete driveway outside the erecting shed, having failed to explode.

As the explosion of the bomb at the position where it rested would have caused considerable damage, its immediate removal was a matter of national importance.

Lieutenant J. M. S. Patton, Royal Canadian Engineers, undertook to remove the bomb to a place of comparative safety and Section Leader Tilyard-Burrows together with Volunteers W. J. Avery, E. A. Maslyn and C. E. Chaplin, with complete disregard of personal safety and having no previous experience of handling unexploded bombs, immediately volunteered to assist.

The bomb was lashed to a sheet of corrugated iron, attached to a truck by wire cable and towed to a crater about 200 yards away where it could do no harm.

The task was accomplished in little more than half-an-hour from the time the bomb had fallen. The bomb exploded the following morning.

Throughout the operation these men displayed cool courage of the highest order and contributed largely to the removal of a serious threat to the production of this factory.

London Gazette.

Lieutenant J. M. S. Patton, Royal Canadian Engineers, was awarded the George Cross.
Captain D. W. C. Cunnington, Royal Canadian Engineers, was awarded the George Medal.
Section Leader A. H. Tilyard-Burrows, Home Guard, was awarded the George Medal.

The George Cross and the George Medal were instituted on 24 September 1940 and were the highest gallantry awards that a civilian could be awarded. At that time it was felt that there was a need to reward people from all walks of life for acts of gallantry.

It was the intention of the authorities that the George Cross should stand supreme and that its position as the 'civilian Victoria Cross' should not be undermined by the award of larger numbers. The result was that the George Medal, was introduced as the second highest civilian gallantry award.

23 September 1940

Heinkel He111
Wn. 3322, 1H+GP, 6./KG26

Location:
West End, Chobham

Time: 01.37 Hours

Crew:
Unteroffizier Karl Niemeyer (27)
(pilot) - baled out safely
Gefreiter Heinrich Leibnitz (20)
(observer) - baled out safely
Gefreiter Stephan Weinlich (26)
(radio operator) - baled out safely
Gefreiter Werner Jenreck (22)
(mechanic) - baled out safely

The authorities keeping watch near Weybridge in the early hours of the morning were stirred to great excitement when parachutes were reported falling. Reports began to come from ARP, firewatchers and other observers as the parachutes were illuminated by searchlights and police and Home Guard set off to round up the Germans.

Three views of the Heinkel wreck at West End, Chobham ....

The Home Guard captured one man at St Georges Hill, a barrage balloon crew at Whitley Village found another man. A third parachutist was quickly arrested in Byfleet, but it was not until half-past-six that the final man was found by the Hersham Police wandering around Burhill Golf Club.

Despite the number of reports of parachutes there were only four men, the crew of a bomber. A few miles away at Chobham a Heinkel had fallen to earth, prompting a search for its crew. Only in the morning did all concerned agree that the two incidents were indeed connected!

The drama had begun three hours earlier when Karl Niemeyer and his crew had taken off from their base Glisy, near to Amiens in France, to attack Beckton Gas Works to the east of London. It was their ninth operational bombing raid and was to be flown alone, with each of the twelve crews navigating and making their way separately to the target.

As he approached London navigator Heinrich Leibnitz began to doubt the accuracy of his own navigation over the blacked-out countryside. A huge fire was clearly visible that he assumed must have been a decoy to lure him away from London, so he ordered his pilot to head west where, twenty-two miles from his intended target, the five 250kg bombs and eight containers of incendiaries were dropped.

A few minutes later the searchlights of 460 Battery, 70th Searchlight Regiment found the Heinkel. Karl Niemeyer turned and dived to throw off the blinding lights, but the searchlight operators held the bomber in the beams long enough for an anti-aircraft battery to open fire and damage it.

Karl Niemeyer gave orders to bale out when he lost control. Mechanic Werner Jehreck was left alone in the cockpit and wrestled with the controls in a desperate attempt to get the aircraft under control, but then decided that he too must bale out.

.... and as it is today - the same houses visible through the trees.

Left to its own devices the Heinkel flew on and hit the ground on an even-keel close to the Gordon Boys' Home at Chobham, where it disintegrated as it bounced and skidded across Guildford Road and Windlesham Road before catching fire.

A BAD BET

ARP MAN MR YEATES REPORTED TO WALTON CONTROL FROM POST B5:

"A thousand pounds to a penny that a 'plane was hit here about 02.00. It went off over in the Sunbury direction labouring badly and I could swear it was coming down."

The day had been forecast to be one of good weather, mostly sunny with a few high clouds. At Fighter Command Headquarters another day of heavy fighting was predicted; for Surrey it would see the last pitched battle of the war.

The first German aircraft overhead were the Bf110s of Lehrgeschwader 1 and Zerstörergeschwader 76, their familiar profiles racing over the countryside in an effort to provoke the defending fighters into the air. In this carefully conceived plan the RAF fighters would be re-fuelling when the second attack took place.

As the Bf110s withdrew the bomber force of fifty-five Junkers Ju88s began their attack, but the plan was already beginning to fall apart. The bombers had been late assembling off the French coast and had missed their rendezvous with the escort of Me109s that should have protected them.

The Ju88s from Kampfgeschwader 77 pressed on and the defending RAF fighters attacked them in force over Kent. Frantic calls from the bombers for fighter support brought the Bf110s back into the fray and by the time the raid reached Surrey a huge and confusing running fight had developed.

Otto Weckeisser's Bf110 down at Oxted with four victory markings on its tail.

Ju 88 crashed at South Holmwood at the same time

Hurri

BRIGHTON LONDON RAILWAY LINE

27th SEPTEMBER 1940

Intense airbattle over North Downs in Surrey 0900hrs when 30 Ju 88s with a big escort were intercepted by eight RAF squadrons. This picture shows where Oblt Baron Ulrich Freiherr von Gravenreuth and his gunner died when their Me 110 was shot down at Gatwick Airport. Dennis Knight

The end of von Gravenreuth's Bf110 at Gatwick. The circular building is Gatwick's original terminal building.
(Dennis Knight)

Sergeant Victor Ekins in a Hurricane from No.501 Squadron was embroiled in a dogfight over Oxted when his aircraft was hit and set alight. He suffered burns, but managed to bail out before his Hurricane dived vertically into the ground at terrific speed.

The largely Polish No.303 Squadron and No.1 (RCAF) Squadron came from Northolt and were soon involved in heavy fighting. Sergeant Joseph Frantisek was credited with bringing down one of the two Lehrgeschwader 1 Bf110s brought down over Surrey. Oberleutnant Ulrich Freiherr von Gravenreuth, the Staffelkapitain of 15/LG1, was chased down to low level and raced over Gatwick aerodrome where his Bf110 was hit by anti-aircraft fire, reared up, and nose-dived into the ground.

Fellow 15./LG1 pilot, Otto Weckeisser, was attacked by seven or eight fighters at 19,000 feet, his gunner was wounded and both his engines put out of action. He was luckier than his Staffel Commander and his crippled machine was escorted down in a most chivalrous manner by three Hurricane pilots, who flew either side and above until he managed to land his aircraft safely near Oxted.

Spitfire pilot Charles Sydney had first attacked the Ju88s near Maidstone, but as the combat became confused he carried on a running fight, chasing the bombers west to the Leatherhead area where another fierce combat developed. Return fire set Sydney's Spitfire alight and he fell to earth at Walton-on-Thames, still in its cockpit. (See page 104.)

27 September 1940

Junkers Ju88A-1
Wn. 8095, 3Z+HK, 2./KG77

Location:
South Holmwood

Time: 09.30 Hours

Crew:
**Unteroffizier Rudolf Schumann (22)
(pilot) - baled out, PoW
Unteroffizier Hans-Joachim Tenholt (28)
(observer) - baled out, PoW
Unteroffizier Wilhelm Menningmann (24)
(W/T) - killed
Unteroffizier Albert Ackermann (26)
(mechanic) - baled out, PoW**

The Ju88 flown by twenty-two year old Rudolf Schumann was singled out by fighters in the same combat at 18,000 feet. The right engine caught fire and the bombs were jettisoned as the fighter attacks continued. The Ju88 dropped out of formation and headed south.

In another attack the left engine caught fire and wireless operator Wilhelm Menningmann baled out; he was seen to drop out of his parachute harness and fall to his death in a meadow near Leatherhead sewage works.

As the stricken bomber flew over Dorking the other three men baled out, leaving the Ju88 to dive vertically into a pasture near South Holmwood where it buried itself in a large crater.

The Ju88 crash at South Holmwood and (left) the pilot, Rudolf Schumann.

303 Squadron lost three aircraft in this morning's combat, one of which crashed in Surrey. This was the Hurricane of Pilot Officer Zak who baled out with burns from a great height during the combat over Leatherhead, leaving his machine to dive into a field at Stoke d'Abernon.

27th Sept 1940 Junkers Ju 88 crashed near Folly Farm, S. Holmwood.
Dennis Knight 1976

27 September 1940

Messerschmitt Bf110D-0
Wn. 3147, L1+BL, 15/LG1

Location:
Gatwick Aerodrome

Time: 09.45 hours
Crew:
Oberleutnant Ulrich Freiherr von Gravenreuth (36) (pilot) - killed
Feldwebel Otto Reinhold (27) - killed

Chased over the airfield by fighters and hit by AA fire.

---

27 September 1940

Messerschmitt Bf110
Wn. 3147, L1+LL, 15/LG1

Location:
Stocketts Manor, Oxted

Time: 09.45 hours
Crew:
Oberleutnant Otto Weckeiser (23) (pilot) unwounded PoW
Gefreiter Horst Brüsgow (22) wounded PoW

Landed after engines failed.

FROM PS CLUTTERBUCK. OXTED POLICE:
'The following fell from a German bomber at 15.20 hours today. Four quick firing guns, together with front and rear turrets, at Tatsfield. Parts fell at Furze Corner and others at Tatsfield Court Farm. Now at Police Cottage Tatsfield.'

---

27 September 1940

Hurricane, V6672
501 Squadron
Location:
North Park Farm, Godstone

Time: 09.15 hours
Pilot:
Sergeant Victor Howard Ekins (26)
baled out, burnt

One of the older Battle Britain pilots at 26 years of age, Victor Ekins had arrived with 111 Squadron at Croydon in early August, straight from training. He made a claim for an Me109 destroyed on 5 September, but when his squadron moved north to rest he was sent to 501 Squadron at Kenley. His Hurricane was hit and set alight by return fire from a Bf110 and he baled out, landing near Sevenoaks with burns. He went on to become an instructor and was given command of 19 Squadron in November 1942; he left the RAF in 1946 from HQ 12 Group.

---

27 September 1940

Hurricane, P3209
73 Squadron
Location:
Galoway's Farm, Monks Holt, Limpsfield

Time: 09.45 hours
Pilot:
Sergeant Peter O'Byrne (23)
climbed out unhurt

This was O'Byrne's first brush with the Surrey countryside, after his Hurricane had been damaged by fire from Bf110s. He crashed again on 29 October.

The excavation of Pilot Officer Zak's Hurricane. Deep in the wreck several oak leaves were found; taken from trees as the fighter crashed through them.

Zak had flown with the pre-war Polish Air Force and made his way to England to join the RAF and 303 (Polish) Squadron based at Northolt.

He made two combat claims before he was shot down on 27 September.

On recovering from his injuries in May 1941 he returned to his squadron at the beginning of a series of appointments; Flight Commander with 303 Squadron, Commanding Officer with 308 Squadron and Wing Leader of the Polish Wing at Kirton-in-Lindsey. He was still in the RAF in 1947 as a Senior Admin Officer and is believed to have died in 1969.

One of the more experienced pilots in the battle, William Smith already had several claims to his credit from combats over Dunkirk and over England. His Hurricane was damaged by return fire from Ju88s and he was obliged to crash land. He crashed again in Surrey on 6 October. He later went to the Middle East, flew with Transport Command, and eventually retired in 1962.

27 September 1940

Spitfire, R6767
92 Squadron
Location:
Station Avenue, Walton-on-Thames

Time: 09.20 hours
Pilot:
Flight Sergeant Charles Sydney (25) killed

One of the most confusing aircraft crashes has been that of Charles Sydney's 92 Squadron Spitfire.

Flying from Biggin Hill, he was variously reported as having crashed at Maidstone and Kingston, but for many years it was believed that his Spitfire had crashed where 'Walton Court' (used by the Unilever Group) now stands close to Walton-on-Thames Railway Station.

A memorial plaque has now been fixed near the building's entrance that is passed by many hundreds of people each day on their dash to or from the station, and an RAF flag is flown from the building during the week preceding Remembrance Day. But the exact site remained a mystery until local historian David Saint took up the challenge to resolve the question once and for all.

In the Surrey History Centre, Woking, he found a bundle of ARP and Fire Brigade messages marked 'Aeroplane Crash 27th September 1940' that gave clues to the real location.

Suggestions as to where the observed falling Spitfire crashed were given variously as; 'Ashley Park towards Weybridge', 'Weybridge Station Area', 'plane down believed British at Cobham', 'one of our aeroplanes has crashed down south of railway line (approx) on allotments (Burwood Park) and from the Esher Report Centre 'One Spitfire down here'. Then from a private phone at 9.28 am. *'St Aubins, Station Avenue, plane down Fire Brigade present'*. An ARP Warden post C7 reported *'St Aubins, Station Avenue. Aeroplane down. Plane all alight. Fire and St John Ambulance representatives on site'*.

But in today's much redeveloped Station Avenue, just where was 'St Aubins'? David Saint then worked with a 1935 map and the 1939 Electoral Register to locate the point where the house once stood, not at the offices at all, but on the other side of Walton Station. The original house called 'St Aubins' has been demolished, as have all but one of the pre-war houses, and a block of garages belonging to the Gainsborough Court Estate now occupies the crash site of Sergeant Sydney's Spitfire.

Charles Sydney joined the RAF in 1930, at 15 years of age, as an apprentice fitter and had volunteered for pilot training when he was old enough. On 27 September he had taken off at 08.45 hours, one of eleven Spitfires ordered to attack

Charles Sydney, the memorial at the Unilever building and the actual crash site; behind the trees at Gainsborough Court.

bombers at 20,000 feet near Maidstone. The formation attacked almost head-on and went straight through the bombers, but then split up and the pilots then found themselves in individual combats and greatly outnumbered by German fighters. No one saw Sydney go down.

He was buried at Orpington on 3rd October, his mother, father and his wife Ellen among the mourners.

30TH SEPTEMBER 1940

The month of September came to a close with a series of half-hearted attacks. The RAF had survived the massed attacks of the past weeks and, despite German propaganda, was still capable of turning the enemy back. Two waves of aircraft flew over Surrey on the afternoon of 30 September and once again the raiders dashed themselves against the Hurricanes and Spitfires.

The sky over south-east England was totally obscured and the combats that were fought took place in the brilliant sunshine high above the clouds. Just after lunchtime two groups of bombers, heavily escorted by Me109s, headed for London. The raid, totalling around 180 aircraft was intercepted over Kent and east Surrey and was dispersed so effectively that very few aircraft made it as far as London. Two of the escorting Messerschmitts fell in the county.

The crash site of Paul Limpert's Messerschmitt near South Nutfield.

---

30 September 1940

Messerschmitt Bf109E-1	**Time: 13.40 hours**
Wn. 4856, 7./JG51	Pilot:
Location:	**Unteroffizier Paul Limpert (20)**
Kentwyns, South Nutfield	**killed**

Shot in the shoulder, baled out too low for the parachute to open and fell by the side of his aircraft.

'The day was overcast and we could hear the sound of fighting above the clouds. After several bursts of machine-gun fire a German fighter dived vertically through the clouds, trailing smoke. The engine was screaming flat out as it went into the ground.

I went over to Wainwright's field where the aircraft had come down only a few yards from the road in a field full of cabbages.

There was a fire and ammunition was popping. A large crowd of people had arrived. The pilot, a young man, was lying some distance from the aircraft, his parachute was out of its pack but I don't think it had opened properly.

His leg was off from just above the knee, he was wearing Jackboots. The dogfight continued above the clouds even after the crash. Two policemen arrived to keep the civilians away.'

Mr Pat Sinclair, interviewed by Dennis Knight in 1960

'Enemy fighter aircraft down and burnt at out 100 yards west of Outwood Road in field at Kentwyns, Parish of Nutfield. Military have taken charge and will remain until relieved. Pilot of 'plane dead please arrange for removal of body.'

Sergeant Beeney, Oxted Police

---

30 September 1940

Messerschmitt Bf109E-1
Wn. 3192, 6./JG52
Location:
Kingswood

Time: 14.00 hours
Pilot:
Gefreiter Gustav Strasser (21)
baled out, severely burned

RAF INTELLIGENCE REPORT

Only identification markings decipherable are a large blue eagle, 4 feet long, on a yellow engine cowling and a yellow tip to the spinner.

Aircraft made by Fieseler Werke Flugzeugwerk in August 1938. Engine DB601A Works No.60337.

According to an eye-witness report, the aircraft was attacked by a Spitfire firing a long burst. An explosion followed and one wing broke off. On crashing the aircraft burnt out.

Armament: Apparently 4 MG17. Armour: Cross bulkhead traced.

"The 'Alert' sounded in Surrey at 09.25 hours and 'All Clear' at 09.50 hours. A second 'Alert' sounded at 13.20 in the Reigate, Banstead area. The weather was warm with 10/10ths high cloud.

Just after 13.30 hours. Mr Bishop with some of his staff left the school buildings where the boys and girls were sheltering and stood in the playground.

Machine-gun fire was heard above the cloud accompanied by the sound of diving aircraft. A single Me109 fell through the cloud in a spin, one wing broke off over Walton Heath, whilst the rest struck the ground at the foot of some trees bordering the heath. The fuselage broke in two and a small fire started with some ammunition exploding. The pilot baled out and drifted down near Ranmore Common.

A 15 cwt truck manned by Canadian soldiers toured roads waiting for him to descend. They eventually took charge of him and rushed him to Dorking General Hospital suffering from considerable burns."

"Mr Killick, the caretaker of the school some 200 yards from where the plane fell, ran to the crashed aircraft intent on procuring a substantial souvenir. He managed to drag the complete tail section some 400 yards across the green to The Blue Anchor Inn. The RAF arrived and there was an exchange of words, later the RAF removed his trophy."

Mr Bishop, Headmaster

"Just off the road on the right were the remains of a German fighter which had wrapped itself around a tree. It might have been something once, but now looked like a heap of tomato cans! The wreck was still smoking, there were a lot of people standing around edging up to the wreckage and trying to pillory souvenirs. The guard warned them away, pointing out that there may be unexploded cartridges or even bombs in the remains. We enquired about the pilot, a woman said he came down at Dorking, several miles away. One of the guards, a Canadian disagrees, 'I think he is still in there' he said, nodding gleefully towards the wreckage."

Harvey Klemmer, US Embassy, published in 'They'll Never Quit'.

The last raid of the day, with over 200 aircraft, headed from Dungeness to Biggin Hill just after 4 o'clock. Like the earlier raid it too was turned back short of its target in running fights from east Kent to the Kenley area. A few raiders continued westward and approached Weybridge, then carried on over west Surrey, Hampshire and West Sussex. Three Luftwaffe aircraft from this raid were shot down in Surrey.

---

30 September 1940

Junkers Ju88A-1
Wn. 2142, 3Z+DK, 2./KG77

Location:
Gatwick Racecourse

Time: 16.30 Hours

Crew:
**Oberleutnant Friedrich Oeser (22) (pilot) - wounded PoW
Gerfreiter Rudi Hülsmann (20) (Observer) - wounded PoW
Oberfeldwebel Gustav Goerke (25) (W/T)- wounded PoW
Unteroffizier Georg Klasing (24) (gunner) - killed**

A hit by anti-aircraft fire on the way to London wounded the pilot, Oberleutnant Oeser, who turned back towards the coast. The already damaged bomber was then set upon by fighters. One engine was hit by gunfire as Oeser tried to escape into the cloud below, but the other engine was then hit. Another burst of machinegun fire struck the crowded cockpit, killing Georg Klasing the gunner and injuring the rest. Seeing that the bomber's fate was sealed the fighter pilots relented and allowed its pilot to make a crash-landing at Gatwick.

Friedrich Oeser's Junkers Ju88 bomber was put on display to raise money for the Spitfire Fund.

30 September 1940

Messerschmitt Bf109E-4
Wn. 5818, Stab JG26
Location:
Hides Farm, Roundhurst

Time: 17.05 hours
Pilot:
**Hauptmann W Kienzle - baled out
seriously wounded PoW**

Attacked by fighters and caught fire. Fell just south of the Surrey border in Sussex.

30 September 1940

Messerschmitt Bf109E-1
Wn. 3859, Yellow 3, 6/JG27
Location:
Holmans Grove, Grayswood

Time: 16.40 hours
Pilot:
**Leutnant Herbert Schmidt - baled out
seriously wounded PoW**

This aircraft was attacked from below when escorting bombers returning from
the London raid. The Daimler-Benz engine caught fire and the pilot baled out
before the aircraft exploded in the air. Herbert Schmidt came down at Fernhurst.

"In the afternoon our Jagdgeschwader was protecting a bomber unit and we got involved in a combat with British fighters. Our formation broke and I chased a Spitfire that dived, while I pulled up the nose of my plane to gain height.

Looking around I was alone, a bad situation for a fighter pilot. It was high time to fly back. Suddenly I saw tracer bullets in my direction of flight, and in the same moment my cockpit was full of flames. A terrible thought flashed through my mind; this is the end!

I tried to release the canopy to get out. I tried to lift my left arm, but it fell by my side; I didn't know that it had been smashed by a bullet. I tried again and again and finally I succeeded in jettisoning the canopy. I couldn't see that, but I felt it because fresh air penetrated the hell of flames I was sitting in. Now I should release my seat harness. I couldn't do it and lost consciousness.

When I recovered my senses I was falling fast, constantly somersaulting. My first idea? I must open the parachute! It was very difficult to pull the handle because my arm was being thrown about as I tumbled, but with a great effort I succeeded in pulling the handle.

When the parachute opened I thought I would be torn to pieces. I was falling fast and nearly all my clothing had been burnt off me. The parachute opened with a jerk and my boots came off.

I floated in the air. I can still picture some things; three Spitfires roaring around and flying away, my blackened and bloody hands, but no feeling of pain.

Something hit my neck, grabbing it I found I had a piece of burning lifejacket in my hand. I tried to beat out the flames with my hands, fearing that the parachute would catch fire and I would hurtle to the ground like a stone. It seemed an eternity before I saw the ground. I made a safe landing, like a real parachutist, near a road and saw two men. They came over to me, 'help' I said, and I heard one say 'badly burned' then – nothing.

The following weeks were the worst of my life, it is a wonder that I am alive, but it wouldn't be right if I didn't mention the British and Canadian doctors and nurses who helped me when I was almost at my end."

Herbert Schmidt

2ND OCTOBER 1940

The air combat, so far as Surrey was concerned, had peaked with the raid on 27 September, after which the enemy only chose to conduct small-scale raids with more Me109s than had been seen before. Such a raid resulted in the two crashes in the north-east of the county on 2 October.

At around ten o'clock fifty bomb-carrying Me109s in three groups headed for the southern outskirts of London and Biggin Hill. Several combats took place and RAF pilots made claims for several enemy aircraft for the loss of a single Spitfire.

South African Peter Dexter had been in combat over the Croydon area with Me109s and claimed to have destroyed one before his Spitfire was hit and he received a wound to a leg. As his aircraft fell Dexter tried to bale out, but found his injured leg trapped in the cockpit by his flying boot. The Spitfire fell 15,000 out of control before he got his foot out of the boot and his parachute opened with just seconds to spare.

---

2 October 1940

Messerschmitt Bf109E-1	**Time: 10.13 hours**
Wn. 6291, Yellow 3, 9./JG53	Pilot:
Location:	**Oberleutnant Walter Radlick**
New Road,	baled out but parachute failed to open.
Limpsfield	**Body found at Hookwood Park.**

---

2 October 1940

Spitfire, P9553	**Time: 10.30 hours**
603 Squadron	Pilot:
Location:	**Pilot Officer Peter Grenfell Dexter (22)**
Still's Farm,	baled out, badly injured.
Addington	**Landed in Featherbed Lane.**

Peter Dexter had joined the RAF in 1938 and flew Lysanders during the Battle of France. In August 1940 he converted to Spitfires at 7 OTU and was operational the following month, making three claims for Me109s before he was shot down and injured.

He returned to operations in April 1941, but was involved in a collision with another Spitfire over the Channel in July and was killed.

3RD OCTOBER 1940

Many of the engagements were now fought closer to the English Channel, which meant a long trip back for the pilots based at the airfields surrounding London, and several pilots were forced to make landings in fields when their fuel ran short.

Oberleutnant Walter Radlick's Me109 left little more than a scar in the ground after the crash.

---

3 October 1940

Hurricane, P3979
213 Squadron
Location:
Rough Beech Farm, Horne

Time: 13.00 hours
Pilot:
Climbed out unhurt.

4TH OCTOBER 1940

Charles English had been on patrol when cloud came down to 200 feet and visibility was about 300 yards. He landed with wheels and flaps down, but his brakes did not work on the wet grass and the aircraft skidded into a hedge.

---

4 October 1940

Hurricane, V6784
UP-E, 605 Squadron
Location:
Pitchfont Farm, Limpsfield

Time: 17.15 hours
Pilot:
Pilot Officer C E English
climbed out unhurt

English had previously claimed two Me109s shot down when flying with 85 Squadron before he moved to Croydon and 605 Squadron on 12 September. Two days after this accident, 7 October, he was shot down over Westerham and died in the wreck of his Hurricane.

6TH OCTOBER 1940

---

6 October 1940

Hurricane, P3716
229 Squadron
Location:
Headley

Time: 14.30 hours
Pilot:
Flying Officer W A Smith (24)
safe.

Landed out of fuel after a patrol (see entry for 27 September)

8TH OCTOBER 1940

Over 150 bombers and fighters headed towards London at around 9 am and were met by a large number of RAF fighters. It was on his return from an engagement over Kent that top scoring ace Josef Frantizek crashed.

A couple of hours later a raid of 'thirty-plus' aircraft crossed the Channel and penetrated to south and east London. Combat was joined with a raid consisting of Ju88s escorted by Me109s over Sussex.

At 11.12 hours Ju88 9K+DM of 4./KG51 was shot down by fighters near Gatwick and crashed at Black Corner, just south of the Surrey border. It exploded and killed all four of the crew.

---

8 October 1940

Hurricane, R4175
303 Squadron
Location:
Cuddington Way, Banstead

Time: 09.40 hours
Pilot:
Sergeant Josef Frantizek (28)
killed

When German forces marched into his native Czechoslovakia in 1938 it is rumoured that Josef Frantizek machine-gunned the troops as he fled for Poland; true or not, it typified his aggressiveness.

He flew in combat during the Polish campaign, then fled to France via Romania, the Balkans and Syria, to join the French Air Force. He is believed to have destroyed eleven enemy aircraft during the Battle of France.

He joined 303 (Polish) Squadron on its formation and at the time of his death he was the highest claiming fighter pilot of the Battle of Britain, with seventeen victories in just five weeks.

He crashed in unexplained circumstances. His Hurricane crash landed on open ground, but when rescuers appeared on the scene he was found to be suffering from serious head injuries, probably sustained when his head hit the gun-sight because his harness was too slack. He may have undone his harness prior to baling out, but then changed his mind, or he may not have realised that the straps were not tight enough to hold him against the sudden deceleration of the crash. He died the day after his 28th birthday.

12TH OCTOBER 1940

Sergeant Josef Frantizek

12 October 1940	
Hurricane, L2101	**Time: 12.55 hours**
615 Squadron, KW-L	Pilot:
Location:	**Pilot Officer E R Edmunds**
Combe Lane, Chiddingfold	**safe**

New Zealander Eric Edmunds was acting a 'weaver' behind his formation when he was attacked by an Me109. A 20mm cannon shell disabled his engine, but he was able to bring his Hurricane in to a safe forced landing.

On 29 October he was shot down and seriously injured over Kent, but recovered and eventually fought over the North African desert where he was shot down for a third time; he became a prisoner of war for the duration.

FOG, CLOUD AND TRAGEDY

The Battle of Britain is often visualised as having taken place in blue skies with, perhaps, some puffy white clouds hiding the winding contrails of the dog-fighting aircraft. There had been days like that, but there had been days of cloud and rain as well.

By mid October the weather had begun to deteriorate, but the men of the RAF had to continue to meet the Luftwaffe. Taking off in poor conditions was the least of the problems for a climb through cloud came next, with an ever-present threat of collision with another aircraft of the squadron. When the pilots broke through the cloud layer into the dazzling clear sky above, the clouds formed a carpet of white and grey that completely obscured the outline of southern England. Now without any reference to the ground navigation became a major problem, particularly so when a chase or combat demanded the pilots' attention.

On return from a patrol the pilots descended into the thick cloud once more, waiting to catch sight of the ground and some landmark that would point the way back to their airfield, hopefully with sufficient fuel to reach it. It is not surprising that with winter approaching losses through accidents began to overtake those caused by combat with the enemy. 14 October proved to be a particularly costly day – and night for the RAF:

14TH OCTOBER 1940

14 October 1940

Hurricane, P3107	Time: 12.45 hours
605 Squadron	Pilot:
Location:	Flying Officer Ralph Hope (27)
Tennison Road, South Norwood	baled out too low - killed

Ralph Hope was a distant relation of Neville Chamberlain and followed the privileged route from Eton to Oxford; rowing for the university in the 1935 Boat Race.

He learned to fly in America when working for the family business and joined 605 Squadron just before the war. He had survived being shot down over Kent on 28 September when he baled out of his Hurricane.

On 14 October he was on a patrol to Hastings from Croydon in 10/10th cloud that extended from 10,000 feet down to just 200 feet above the ground. The precise circumstances of his loss are a mystery, but in the heavy cloud he missed Croydon airfield and strayed into the Inner Artillery Zone that protected London. Here his Hurricane either struck a balloon cable or he was hit by anti-aircraft fire. His 'plane fell on allotments in South Norwood, but Ralph Hope's body was discovered half a mile away with an unopened parachute.

He had a wife, Dianna, and was cremated at Woking Crematorium.

14 October 1940

Whitley, P4993
ZA-V, 10 Squadron

Location:
Hangar Hill, Weybridge

Time: 20.00 hours

Crew:
**Pilot Officer Kenneth Cooney (24)
(pilot) - killed
Sergeant Dennis Raymond Wright (20)
(pilot) - killed
Sergeant James John Caswell
(observer) - killed
Sergeant Edward Davies (18)
(wireless operator) - killed
Sergeant Bert Llewellyn Henry (19)
(gunner) - killed**

Took off from Leeming for Le Havre. Hit balloon barrage.

Sergeant Wright's crew was one of the three from No.10 Squadron based at Leeming in Yorkshire detailed to attack Le Havre. They took off at 17.31 hours and headed south, on a course that should have taken them to the west of London's anti-aircraft defences, but all was not going according to plan.

On the ground near Weybridge in Surrey observers saw coloured flares fired from an aircraft, then cheered as it fell to the ground in flames. At last the defences of Brooklands had taken revenge for the terrible raid on its aircraft factory that had

A Whitley from 10 Squadron, similar to the bomber that crashed on Hangar Hill.

116

taken place on 4 September. When the first of the five bodies was found the terrible truth dawned; they had brought down an RAF bomber.

The Whitley had flown into a balloon cable flown from Site 21, which had severed a wing. A subsequent investigation determined that incendiaries had ignited in the bomb bay, but whether this occurred before or after hitting the cable was not known. The wing fell at Weybridge Park, the tail unit with the rear turret fell onto a house named Elgin Lodge in Elgin Road, the rest of the aircraft exploded in flames at Hangar Hill near the railway embankment close to Weybridge station.

Eighty-one year old Thomas Dickson was living in Elgin Lodge with his wife and staff and wrote the following account which was provided by the family to researcher Stephen Flower for his book *Raiders Overhead*:

Elgin Lodge was patched up with a tarpaulin over the roof, but the occupants would have had an uncomfortable winter.

In June 1941 Thomas Dickson, veteran of the Boer War and First War, heard the air raid sirens sound again. He rose suddenly from his bed, and died of a stroke.

There is nothing left today to mark the tragedy. A block of flats stands in Elgin Road where the Lodge once stood and each day hundreds of commuters pass by the crash site on their way to the station bound for London.

At Elgin Lodge we have so far been fortunate in escaping any injury by the enemy bombers, although every night they make great efforts all round us to get armament works near this.

However, on Monday the 14th the house was severely damaged, not by the enemy, but, alas, by one of our own bombers.

Mrs Dickson, Miss Niven and I dine at seven pm. The enemy is generally overhead by seven-thirty. We had finished and were in the drawing room before a good fire. We usually, when the explosions get dangerously near, shut up and retire to our cellar shelter, where we are safe against anything but a direct hit, and sleep in good cabin bunks with the staff: five in all.

We were just deciding to get down to our shelter when there was a fearful crash, with a crescendo of falling glass, and the whole house trembled. We all got down to the shelter in thirty seconds and waited, while bomb after bomb exploded close by. After ten minutes the explosions ceased and the parlour maid, who is fearless, went up to see what had happened. She came back and waved her hand to me, but said nothing.

I went upstairs to the large bedroom, where Mrs Dickson and I sleep in peacetime. The door could only be opened a few inches, but enough to show me the room piled with wreckage, a large hole in the ceiling and floor above, and a larger one in the roof above that, with the moon shining in a clear sky.

As there had been no explosion in the house, I concluded that a delayed-action bomb had struck us. I at once went out to get help and luckily found a flight lieutenant and three Army officers and a couple of cars waiting at the end of Elgin Road. They offered their services, and one of the RAF men said he would have a look outside before going upstairs, produced his torch, and in a moment said, 'Well, you have had an escape, your house has been hit by an aeroplane, and only the lightest part of it.'

Next day we learned what had happened. A British Whitley two-engined bomber had evidently left to attack the French coast, but developed engine trouble which forced the pilot to return without dropping his bombs. He was seen in difficulties, flying low round St. George's Hill, evidently seeking a landing place.

Unfortunately, he fouled a balloon cable, dropped both wings in different places; engines and bombs fell on the commons, burnt themselves out and exploded the bombs. The tailpiece and turret with four machine guns and full load of cartridges carried on and cut into the Elgin Lodge roof, scraped off the turret guns and cartridges, weighing nearly a ton, leaving it on Mrs Dickson's bed, and landed on the tennis court, carrying the drawing-room veranda with it. The crew of five were all killed. They hadn't a dog's chance; they were too low down to allow their parachutes to open and their dead bodies were found in various directions.

Sentries were put on the wreckage at once. The corporal slept in a chair in the hall. Next morning, from daylight numberless inspectors, officers, wardens and others came to look at the wreckage. It was only then that the machine was identified and it was not until the same evening that the last of the dead was found.

17TH October

Today the RAF salvage officers and men arrived from Slough and have been dismantling, collecting, packing and laying out every nut, bolt and instrument. The turret, a mass of intricate machinery, is being cut and dismembered piece by piece; belts containing thousands of unexploded cartridges and four machine guns packed into sacks and hoisted from off Mrs Dickson's bed, to be lowered from the window.

It is rather a sad business to find gauntlets, oxygen masks, emergency rations belonging to the dead crew with their names on them among the wreckage.

Thomas Dickson

---

14 October 1940

Beaufighter If, R2079
219 Squadron
Location:
Tannery Lane, Send

Time: 00.50 hours

Crew:
Both baled out safely

The Bristol Beaufighter was a new addition in Fighter Command's arsenal to counter the night bombing offensive of the Luftwaffe. By October 1940 very few were in service and each machine was considered to be a valuable asset, particularly now that winter was approaching and that enemy tactics had changed to a series of large-scale night attacks.

The Beaufighter, first line of defence against the Luftwaffe's night Blitz.

Night flying was never easy when over a blacked-out countryside and radio communication with the ground was vital. On this night the radio failed and the pilot was attempting to find Fairoaks airfield in bad visibility when the fuel began to run low. The crew, whose names are not recorded, baled out safely leaving the brand new night fighter to its fate.

15 October 1940

Hurricane, V6722	Time: 08.15 hours
501 Squadron	Pilot:
Location:	**Sergeant Stanley Allen Fenemore** (20)
Postern Gate Farm, South Godstone	**killed**

Shot down by Me109s over Redhill – Godstone area.

FENEMORE ROAD

SERGEANT STANLEY ALLEN FENEMORE
HURRICANE PILOT 501 SQUADRON R(Aux)AF
KILLED IN ACTION 15TH OCTOBER 1940 AGED 20
"ONE OF THE FEW"

Fair weather heralded a day of much increased activity, with over 500 enemy aircraft roaming over England during the day. At 8 o'clock three raids totalling about fifty aircraft flew in over Dover and Dungeness, went as far as the southern outskirts of London and then retired.

The Hurricanes of 501 Squadron intercepted the raiders leading to the loss of Sergeant Fenemore, whose Hurricane was seen diving to the ground near South Godstone.

Irishman Stanley Fenemore from Co. Antrim had a short career. After joining the RAF in February 1939 and initial training he leaned fighter tactics at 5 Operational Training Unit between May and July 1940.

After a few weeks with 245 Squadron, then stationed in the Irish backwater of Aldergrove, he joined the fray with 501 Squadron at Kenley in September.

On 15 October, in one of his first combats, his Hurricane was shot down by an Me109 and dived into the ground taking its young pilot to his death.

Sergeant Stan Fenemore, now honoured by a road on the new estate at Kenley named after him.

> ## 16 October 1940
>
> ### Blenheim Mklf, L1236
> **219 Squadron**
> Location:
> **Redhill Airfield**
>
> ### Time: 09.50 hours
> Pilot:
> **Sergeant H Grubb**
> **safe**
>
> **Returning from a patrol the pilot tried to land, but he opened throttles to jump over a muddy patch created by contractor's vehicles driving over the grass and was unable to stop before he hit the boundary. The Blenheim was repairable.**

18TH OCTOBER 1940

The Poles of the newly formed 302 Squadron and their English instructors.

Once again terrible flying conditions lead to the loss of men and aircraft in Surrey. A flight from 302 Squadron, based at Northolt, had been sent to patrol north Kent as poor weather closed in.

One member of the flight is believed to have attempted to land at Detling, but his aircraft flew into a hill and he was killed.

The remainder of the flight found their way back over Surrey and were in the vicinity of Brooklands when the next tragedy struck. The barrage balloons were flying in defence of the aircraft factory that had suffered so badly in the 4 September raid and it is believed that Stefan Wapniarek's Hurricane struck one of these cables, sending his Hurricane spinning to the ground.

Moments later two more Hurricanes fell to earth near Kempton Park race course. One of these pilots, Carter, was experienced but the other had only joined the squadron the day before, straight from training. Although it has often been recorded that the aircraft crashed when trying to land, witnesses have said that the planes fell at steep angles and exploded on hitting the ground, leading to the conclusion that the two aircraft collided in the poor visibility.

---

18 October 1940

Hurricane, P3872
302 Squadron, WX-R
Location:
Norwood Farm, Cobham

Time: 16.05 hours
Pilot:
**Pilot Officer Stefan Wapniarek (24)
killed**

May have hit balloon cable in cloud.

Stefan Wapniarek had fought over Poland and had shot down three German aircraft. He made his way to England, joined 302 Squadron in July 1940 and shot down a Ju88 on 18 September.

---

18 October 1940

Hurricane, P3930
302 Squadron, WX-X
Location:
Kempton Park Racecourse

Time: 16.05 hours
Pilot:
**Pilot Officer Jan Borowski (28)
killed in his aircraft**

Another pilot to pass through 5 OTU at Aston Down was Jan Borowski. He arrived at Northolt to join 302 Squadron on 17 October, but was killed the next day on his first flight.

---

18 October 1940

Hurricane, P3931
302 Squadron WX-V
Location:
Kempton Park Racecourse

Time: 16.05 hours
Pilot:
**Pilot Officer Peter Edward George Carter
(21) - baled out too low - killed**

Peter Carter had flown with 73 Squadron in France and claimed to have brought down two Ju88s on 15 August. He was then attached to the Polish 302 Squadron to assist the squadron in becoming operational.

22ND OCTOBER 1940

Fog and rain persisted in the morning and kept most aircraft of both sides on the ground until the afternoon when about thirty Me109s flew to Redhill, circled, and then headed back. One Spitfire was seen to fall out of the clouds and dive into the ground with its pilot still in the cockpit.

22 October 1940

Spitfire IIa, P7431
74 Squadron
Location:
**Cornmongers Farm, Cooper's Hill,
South Nutfield**

Time: 14.05 hours
Pilot:
**Flying Officer Peter Cape Beauchamp
St. John - killed**

An excavation carried out at the crash site of Stefan Wapniarek's Hurricane in the late 1970s.

Pilot Officer Peter Carter

Flying Officer Peter St. John.

22 October 1940

Hurricane, V6783
605 Squadron, WX-X
Location:
Landbarn Farm, Dorking

Time: 14.30 hours
Pilot:
Pilot Officer John A Milne (25)
broken hip

Canadian born John Milne had shot down a Bf110 on 27 September, but on this day his Hurricane was damaged by Me109s over Croydon and he elected to make a crash landing. The fighter hit the ground so heavily that Milne's hip was broken and he spent several weeks in hospital, where he met a nurse who he later married. He survived the war and returned to Canada in 1946.

25TH OCTOBER 1940

25 October 1940

Spitfire IIa, P7442
41 Squadron
Location:
Tandridge Lodge, Tandridge

Time: 16.30 hours
Pilot:
Pilot Officer John Noble Mackenzie (26)
safe

Landed out of fuel and repaired.

John Mackenzie sailed from New Zealand in 1937 to join the RAF. He became a successful fighter pilot and flew throughout the Battle of Britain. On 25 October he damaged two Me109s, then ran out of fuel and crash-landed.

27TH OCTOBER 1940

During the morning around 60 aircraft flew to the Kenley and Biggin Hill areas, with ten getting as far as Central London. Fourteen squadrons were sent up and six Me109s were destroyed, two of them in Surrey.

27 October 1940

Messerschmitt Bf109E-4
Wn.1268, Black 5, 2./JG52
Location:
East Park House, Newchapel

Time: 09.25 hours
Pilot:
Gefreiter Carl Bott (20)
baled out safely PoW

Shot down by Flight Lieutenat McKellar of 605 Squadron.

An Me109 makes its way along the coast during the Battle of Britain period.

Carl Bott was training to be an infantryman at the outbreak of the war, but in November 1939 he transferred to a flying school at Pilsen where he learnt to fly.

At the end of May 1940 he moved to a fighter pilots' school where he flew Me109s for up to three hours a day with 60 other trainees, two of whom were killed in flying accidents.

At the end of August he was posted to the training Staffel of Jagdgeschwader 52 to prepare for operations with 2./JG52. On the morning of 27 October he was ready for his first – and last - combat flight over England. The RAF interrogation officers reported:

"Start and Mission: Started from a field aerodrome near Calais at 07.30 hours on a freelance patrol.

"This pilot, who had only recently joined his unit, took off with Oberleutnant Lehmann on a 'freelance' patrol, which was to be his initiation into operational flying.

"His only previous experience had been two practice flights, during which he flew as far as Dover, but encountered neither British aircraft, nor AA fire.

"On the present flight, they flew at 28,000 feet at a speed of 500 to 550 kilometres per hour, with a following wind. The two aircraft had been flying for nearly an hour, when three Spitfires were noticed close behind them, and a fourth attacked this aircraft from the starboard beam, hitting the engine, and smashing the

oil feed. The cockpit was soon full of smoke, and the pilot baled out at 5,000 feet. The aircraft crashed, and was smashed into small pieces.

"Morale: Not good. Rather nervous and very talkative, but did not appear to know very much of value. Thought Germany would win, but hoped there would be peace negotiations soon, as he was sick of the war."

---

27 October 1940

Messerschmitt Bf109E-7
Wn.4124, Stab I/JG3
Location:
Wickham Court Farm,
Addington

Time: 12.00 hours
Pilot:
Leutnant Wilhelm Busch
baled out safely at New Addington
where he was rescued from irate
housewives by soldiers

Whilst the housewives were chasing the pilot, the sons and husbands gathered around the wreckage of Busch's Me109 looking for souvenirs!

---

27 October 1940

Spitfire IIa, R6721
92 Squadron
Location:
Norbury Park, Mickleham

Time: 11.15 hours
Pilot:
Sergeant Donald Ernest Kingaby (20)
safe

Landed out of fuel and repaired.

Don Kingaby (far right) was later described in newspapers as 'the 109 specialist' and flew throughout the war, leaving the RAF as a Wing Commander.

29TH OCTOBER 1940

---

29 October 1940

Hurricane, V7595
501 Squadron
Location:
Leatherhead

Time: 14.15 hours
Pilot:
Sergeant Peter O'Byrne (23)
safe

Peter O'Byrne had already had a brush with the Surrey countryside when he crash-landed on 27 September at Limpsfield. This time his engine failed during formation flying at 12,000 feet from Kenley and he tried to land in a field that had stakes to stop enemy aircraft landing, but overshot and crashed into a wood. The Commanding Officer's view was that he should have glided back to base, which should have been possible from that height.

After the Battle of Britain he was posted the Middle East, then flew Dakotas over Yugoslavia to drop supplies to partisans and ended the war in Burma and India.

On leaving the RAF in 1946 O'Byrne became an airline captain, flying with Aer Lingus and Jersey Airlines, until he retired.

---

29 October 1940

Hurricane, P3085
302 Squadron
Location:
Chobham

Time: 15.30 hours
Pilot:
Flight Lieutenant James Anderson
Thomson (24) - baled out injured

James Thomson had been posted to the newly formed 302 Squadron in July 1940 as a flight commander. On 29th October he collided with Hurricane V6923 flown by Flight Lieutenant Czerny during a routine patrol over Brooklands and baled out. Thomson was later posted to the Far East and ended the war with the rank of wing commander.

And so the 'Battle of Britain' came to an end; not with a climactic battle, but a gradual decline in the fighting. The RAF fighter pilots 'The Few' together with gunners and the countless men and women on the ground had prevented the Luftwaffe gaining air supremacy and thus prevented an invasion of Britain.

But the Luftwaffe never recognised the 'Battle of Britain' in that way; rather, it denoted a phase in their assault and heralded a change in tactic. The RAF had not been defeated by the knock-out blows against airfields like Kenley, the phalanx of bombers had been turned away from London and the worsening weather made further operations difficult. Replacement crews and aircraft were arriving at airfields in occupied Europe every day. Occasional missions were flown over Britain in November and December 1940, but the massed armadas of bombers were never to be seen over England again.

1941 saw the coming of the next phase in the Luftwaffe's attack on Britain - the night Blitz. The Spitfires and Hurricanes that had defended Britain's cities so successfully were all but powerless against the night bombers, faith had to be put in the new technology of Airborne Interception 'Radar'. The skies over Surrey echoed to a new sound, the twin engines of the night fighting Beaufighters. New heroes emerged, like 'Cat's Eyes' Cunningham, and once again Surrey was in the Front Line, standing in the path of the Luftwaffe.

Whyteleafe cemetery, where many who flew from Kenley now rest.

'Surely the most beautiful of all churchyards'
'Dutch' Hugo, 615 Squadron